CLIMBING
WITH SASHA,
a Washington Husky

❖

Warren Guntheroth

Published by
  Husky Books
  PO Box 27803
  Seattle WA 98125-2803

Front cover and page 9: The Princess in her native element.
  Photo by Ellie Guntheroth.
Back cover: Photo by Ed Emery.

Book design and layout by
  Pack & Paddle Publishing, Inc
  PO Box 1063
  Port Orchard WA 98366

ISBN 0-9636921-2-7

 This book is produced in the USA
with recycled paper.

❖ CONTENTS ❖

AUTHOR'S NOTE

❖

I was born in the flatlands of mid-America. Actually, Hominy, Oklahoma, has rolling hills and is not all that flat, but no one calls the hills "mountains," even though the Ozark Mountains are not far away. Snow is a four-letter word that describes a rare and evanescent event in that part of the world.

I attended Will Rogers High School in Tulsa, and was best known for playing the bass in the swing band and dating Eddie Lou. I was a closet scholar, and there was open disbelief when I announced that I was leaving Tulsa for Harvard College. I had no particular interest in the mountains of New England, but I did have a job that developed some useful skills: I delivered *The Crimson* each morning, which required climbing up and down 123 flights of stairs before breakfast.

I crossed the Charles River to Boston to attend Harvard Medical School. During my senior year I did have one brief ski outing in the Laurentians with Poppy, but there was simply no time for all that!

After my internship and residency, there *was* time for marriage to Ellie, and not long thereafter, a trip west to Seattle. During the early years, I had no time for entertainment, although I did manage three boys, Kurt, Karl, and Sten. I knew there were mountains nearby, because at least once a year the clouds parted, and there they were!

It finally occurred to me that there was little reason to put up with the low salary at the University of Washington and the miserable weather if I wasn't actively involved in the surroundings of this emerald city. After a disastrous outing to fish in a high lake with Harvey, a neighbor, I decided I should at least learn survival skills, and signed up for a climbing course (non-credit, of course) at the University of Washington. I became hooked!

The same year, my wife decided to go to Sun Valley, with or

without me. With incredible perception, I sensed a threat to my marriage. I went, and learned how to really ski, and to rediscover Ellie.

It wasn't long before I climbed and skied regularly with my "classmate" Ed Emery. It is a great convenience not having to commit to a formal schedule when the weather is as unpredictable as it is in Seattle, particularly early on a Saturday morning when you can hear the rain pounding the roof. How nice to crawl back into a warm bed after a quick call to your partner.

I work at the medical school as a pediatric cardiologist and in my "spare time" I do research, teach physiology, and have written three medical textbooks and 210 papers in medical journals. I began writing about Sasha as a result of a contest in The Mountaineers' monthly publication. My entry was in the category of "the Best of Climbs," which appears here as "Sasha's first night out."

At 68, I have climbed 433 peaks, including the tallest 25 in the state of Washington, and a first ascent of Alaska's Mount Lodge just last year. I can do serpentines in powder snow and Telemark turns on nordic skis. Sasha, a *much* younger female, has climbed 188 peaks and doesn't need skis! Together, we spend 60 days a year in the mountains.

Warren Guntheroth
Seattle, Washington
October 1995

1

❖ THE ABDUCTION ❖

Phil was enrolled in my class in a non-credit course in mountaineering taught at the University of Washington, back when they could get insurance for such activities. This class graduated a surprising number who continued to climb in the next few years, and Phil was the best at the vertical stuff. One of the most memorable climbs he and I attempted was Outer Space, a 5.9 climb on Snow Creek Wall, a magnificent piece of granite near Leavenworth, Washington. It was a long climb, in part because it occurred before the introduction of jam nuts made of alloys; protection from falls at that time required pounding in giant angle-pitons, called "bongs" because of the sound they make when they are hammered in. Phil led off with confidence.

The worst part of the route rounded a tall pillar that prevented hearing each other, which led to 30 minutes of both of us waiting tensely, holding on to our respective ends of the climbing rope, thinking the other was in some desperate circumstance, and might fall at any second. Finally, Phil tied off his end of the rope and climbed down on my side of the pillar until I could hear him.

It was a hot day, and we drank the last of our water about five o'clock, and then grey and black clouds slowly moved in, threatening us with rain and worse—lightning. Although motivated by the dangers of finishing a technical climb in these conditions, it still took until 10pm to reach the top and we had to descend the hospitable trail by flashlight.

It is not easy to explain why this is entertaining, but I continue to relish the sport after 30 years, and it was disappointing when Phil dropped out not long after Outer Space. Phil did continue hiking in the mountains, but confined his outings to high lake fishing. However, after a few years, Phil called and told me he had a new dog, Ulu, a Siberian husky, and suggested a climb with her. She was quite different from Sigi, our German shepherd, who was very intelligent, but not at all fond of heights, and whose hind limbs were pathetically weak.

Ulu was also different vocally; when Phil and I reached some minor cliffs, he tied her in the shade of a large granite boulder and we went on toward the summit. It was an idyllic spot, with water and soft grass shaded by the boulder, but she announced loudly to all in the valley of Monte Cristo that she was being torn limb from limb. I have yet to hear more varied or louder howls and sobs. Fortunately, the summit was not far, although there was a final difficult pitch. I was secretly pleased that Phil was no longer confident on the vertical face, and I led it with relish.

Phil did not give me any other opportunities to lead; he again retired from climbing in favor of hiking with Ulu, and I heard little from him for the next two or three years. Then he announced that Ulu had delivered a handsome pack of pups who were being snapped up at a great pace, and offered us a chance to learn about Siberian huskies firsthand. My wife, Ellie, argued that she had had enough of staying home on weekends while I climbed, taking care of our boys, now graduated, and dogs. (Sigi had died an unpleasant death of cancer.) Phil knew his product, however, and brought out the entire litter when they were three months old, and Ellie's stoney resolve almost melted. But not quite.

Another three years passed, and Phil called again with the news that Ulu was again expecting and this would be her last litter since she was eight years old. Ellie and I agonized, since we both missed a canine presence. Our cat Snidely was nice enough, but only a cat. Yet it didn't seem quite fair to Ellie, and I did not insist. This time though, we took the ferry over to Bainbridge Island, just to admire Phil's pups and to see what we would miss.

Ulu weighed at least 50 pounds, and had a completely white face, except for the usual black around her eyes and the black head and ears. She was somewhat aloof, for those of us not in the immediate family. Her mate was Max, a gentleman lovable to the point of neurosis. Max belonged to Jeanne, who swears that Phil married her for her dog. (Actually, Jeanne produced a single litter of a remarkable boy who completely captured Phil's heart.)

There were only four pups in Ulu's litter. There was a rust colored girl, another girl that resembled Ulu, and two pups that looked very much like Max, a terribly handsome guy. These two pups, one boy and one girl, were the liveliest of the litter, which, if you know about the breed, is not necessarily a selling point. Ellie observed that she certainly wasn't up to taking care of a pup as active and aggressive as the male, and at that point the female demonstrated that she was a natural athlete by being the only one of the litter to jump onto the couch.

That jump sealed our fate, and we left with this dynamo with the pale blue eyes, tall pointed ears with a delicate pink on the inside, and a face that is prettier than I have seen in any four legged creature. (An orca whale or a penguin might compete with her, since they too have the look of someone dressed formally in black and white, ready for a night out.) The back of her head and ears are jet black, but the white mask extends well above her eyes, which are lined with black, giving the impression of a carefully prepared geisha. Two thin black lines go down her muzzle to her surprisingly mobile nose, separated by a thin white stripe that extends well up her forehead. Her ears are almost always at full alert, except for extraordinarily rare instances of remorse, or when she runs at top speed when they lay back in a stylish streamline.

Her back is quite black and her chest and legs are white, with a transition from white to black on her sides, forming subtle cornrows. Her tail is the only part of her that is less than perfect. There is a point a few inches from her fluffy bottom where the tail seems to straighten out a little, causing her to carry it in an arc, but not the complete circle common to her brother and sisters. This

13

A defiant three-month-old glaring at her step-mother: "I don't have to because you're not my real mother."

tail also seemed to be exquisitely sensitive; her brother Woot capitalized on this, and frequently tried to pull her out from under chairs by this extremity. Her piercing cries instantly reminded me of her mother's screams a few years earlier in the mountains. They were also the prelude to an epic first night.

Phil and Jeanne supplied us with an old sock that was Sasha's favorite, and the drive and ferry ride across Puget Sound was deceptively peaceful. She explored our house quickly, tested its water-resistant qualities, and failed to find suitable constituents for a pack. It quickly became obvious to her that she was a victim of pupnapping, and her indignation was apparent. She would have nothing to do with us, but sat forelegs wide apart, and with a defiant frown. She glared at Ellie with a strong message: "You're not my mother, and I don't *have* to!"

As night fell, she became more anxious. She began vocalizing early, and when we went to bed we put her in the basement bathroom with as many comforting things as we could imagine. Our bedroom was up two flights, and we had two closed doors and a long corridor between us and Sasha, but that was as nothing. Our surprise at the loudness of this distressed pup gave way to amazement at the legendary stamina of the husky breed—there was not a single moment of quiet during the long night.

In addition to a remarkable vocabulary, she could be heard hurling herself at the closed door, and making miscellaneous sounds that seemed life-threatening. Neither Ellie nor I really slept, and the next morning we confessed that we each harbored dark thoughts of "back to the puppy farm," thoughts that recurred frequently for the next year.

The resilience of both Sasha and her step-parents emerged with the dawn, and we decided that, since Sasha was not inclined in the least to compromise, we would have to if the relationship was to survive. Ellie found a suitable-sized cardboard box and placed it next to our bed, where she could reach down and comfort Sasha during the night if she cried. Although the quality of our sleep the second night could not truthfully be described as good, it was so much better than the first night that Sasha did not get banished to the puppy farm, but sleeps at our bedside to this day, on her very own mattress.

2

❖ ESCAPE! ❖

Phil had approached the rearing of Ulu in the careful manner of any new parent by reading the closest thing to Doctor Spock he could find. He knew every charming characteristic of the breed, and had entertained me with stories about Siberian huskies' legendary stamina during our earlier climb. Looking back, I can vouch for his veracity, as far as he went, but I was far from fully informed. (As any reasonable spouse knows, any union is more serene if some information is not volunteered.)

Later, when asked about some less desirable trait of our Sasha, he would softly agree that he too had experienced that, but reassured us that this phase would pass quickly. However, the duration of puppy rebellion in this breed could be described as brief by only the most hopelessly optimistic owner. I can't recall a single warning from Phil about what we were in for—I can only be grateful that he doesn't sell automobiles. Still, if he had, we would undoubtedly come to love our car as we have come to love this little wolf-dog.

The title of wolf is not a casual one. The family of dogs includes two main branches, *Canis aureus* and *Canis lupus*, and the husky is firmly in the camp of *lupus*, Latin for wolf. The behavior of these two branches of dogs are strikingly different, described by

Konrad Lorenz in a delightful book, *King Solomon's Ring*, in 1950. (The title concerns the ring that, when worn, permitted Solomon to talk to animals; the book is a study of animal behavior.)

Anyone who deigns to associate with a husky as a prospective alpha-person would do well to read at least the chapter, "The Covenant." Ellie read this to me in bed over the period of several evenings. Lorenz' description of the behavior of these wolf-dogs was simply astounding to us—it was as though he were describing Sasha, individually.

He warned of a behavior that is both a never-ending challenge and eventually a source of pride to the owner adequately trained by his dog: this breed "is, in spite of his boundless loyalty and affection, never quite sufficiently submissive. He is ready to die for you, but not obey you." It is clear that Lorenz preferred this lupus-dog to the totally domesticated dog with its "infantile affection" and mindless obedience.

Although we chuckled as we read of the proud heritage of Sasha, the reality of this struggle for the alpha position in our pack was less amusing. There were the usual puppy-type destructive assaults on slippers, shoes, the automobile interior, and the deck railing. But her most annoying and dangerous obsession was the unaccompanied exploration of her environs, which had no finite boundaries.

Taking her out for a potty break was followed by her casually trotting away down the driveway toward adventure. (Running away was attributed to a desire for socialization more than adventure by Elizabeth Marshall Thomas, although her hero, Mischa, seemed to have adequate canine companionship at home.) If Sasha was sternly commanded, "Sasha come!" she would acknowledge the command by a glance over her shoulder, with not the slightest hint of remorse or hesitation. She was not trying to leave us, since she always returned after some hours, but her curiosity about what was out there was intense.

I know of no one who is owned by this breed who has not experienced the battle of keeping these pups at home; they are talented at jumping fences and indefatigable at digging under them. It did not take long for us to conclude that we needed a strong and tall fence, with the bottom buried under 12 inches of gravel. However, that did not solve the potty-break issue, since she regarded the small fenced-in area as inappropriate for this function. To avoid the runaway scene, she had to be taken out the front door on a leash, no matter the weather, or how much of a hurry we were in, or how reassuring Sasha was that she had no interest in anything but evacuation of bowel or bladder.

The wanderlust was controlled somewhat by installing a long steel wire with a light rope attached by a sliding loop, which gave her some freedom to use the undeveloped rear of our lot. Although she was surprisingly successful at avoiding wrapping the rope around the numerous obstacles, in the course of an entire afternoon she would usually wind up entangled on one of them.

She quickly learned not to tire herself in vain attempts to unwind, but would bark once to call her servant, and then lie down. There was little ambiguity about her bark since she almost never barked at strangers, either animal or human. (Although this may suggest an inadequate devotion to the role of watchdog, her unfailing attention to her immediate environment keeps her well informed of visitors, including even birds and airplanes. It is only necessary to glance at her to know that somebody or something unusual is nearby.)

Her alertness for escape opportunities contributed to the problem of keeping her off the street. Although we live on a secluded street, speeding automobiles are not rare, and their danger is increased by Sasha's conviction that, since cars are driven by humans, they could not possibly hurt her, since all humans admire her.

After installing the fence and the wire, our next strategy for containment was to enroll Sasha in obedience training. Her intelligence made her an excellent student, and she won the award for the "most improved" member of the class. Ellie diligently practiced outside the class with Sasha, and there were occasional brief sessions with me, but Sasha seemed to have memorized Lorenz' description of the breed's independence.

It was, in short, a guilt-free puppy that took over our house. The first five months passed without a single instance in which Sasha displayed any emotion that could remotely be considered remorse, even after corporal punishment.

The turning point was a spring night at 10pm when our company was leaving after a relaxing dinner. As usual, the last minute exchanges took place at the front door, and Sasha quietly edged toward the opening, and then quickly escaped down the stairs and straight down the driveway. Ellie and I followed down the driveway, then walked in opposite directions up and down the street for half an hour, calling softly, but without result. We finally went to bed, but left the front door slightly ajar. At midnight, the front door banged open, and Sasha trotted up the stairs to our bedroom. She quickly circled the bed to make sure *we* were secure, and then raced me to the door, making good her second escape. This routine was repeated at one o'clock and two o'clock.

At about three, I heard a single bark, followed by an ominous screech of tires on the street below our driveway, accompanied by the sound of teenagers swearing. With a heavy heart, I got up, dressed, and went down to retrieve the body. I was greatly relieved to find her intact, but more than a little annoyed to see her sitting serenely in our turn-around, chewing on a bag of fish food she had stolen from a neighbor's porch. She seemed surprised when I seized her by the collar and hauled her into the house.

One of the most difficult dilemmas in training dogs is how to discipline them when they do not come to your command. If you administer the punishment when they do come, an unfortunate association is established. However, to administer the punishment when they are in the act of running away requires that you catch them first, and with a pup such as Sasha, that was no trivial requirement.

Our consultant, who had taught the obedience class, suggested a remote-control electronic training collar. Our first response was that such an approach seemed too severe. However, the prospect of our pup being run over seemed considerably more brutal; our decision that next morning after the great escape was unanimous: *The Collar!* (Sasha was asleep at the time of the vote). Initially, we simply rented the device, a radio-controlled unit bolted onto a regular collar, with a stimulus intensity that could be adjusted.

That first morning after *The Collar* was activated when she crossed the white string boundary Ellie rigged around our property line, and the remote button was pushed, she instantly stopped, and promptly retreated to areas on the home side of the line. Sasha is a *very* quick study, and she knew at once that she had encountered some mysterious and powerful medicine!

It required only two shocks at home, and one at the park to convince her that, although we otherwise did not earn the honor, our powerful lightning entitled us to the alpha-position. Still, she also deduced that the lightning was in *The Collar*, and not in her regular collar decorated with name and license tag. This required the rental of the apparatus again after a few weeks, and eventually the purchase of the kit, including a dummy collar that looked and weighed the same as *The Collar*.

We were happy that it did not require the administration of an actual shock to remind her to come—simply attaching the dummy collar was sufficient. However, we have learned to respect her characteristic behavior of a brief hesitation before she responds to our commands; perhaps we found such behavior familiar, after rearing three adolescents.

Lorenz described this husky attitude well: they *will* respond, but their covenant with us requires a respect for their disdain for the instantaneous response of an Irish setter, or other *Canis aureus* breeds. As with children, discipline is essential for normal development. Our goal for Sasha was not mindless submission, but to prepare her for a world that is less tolerant than her parents. Of course, as in every family, there is one who preaches the rewards of discipline, and one who is a "soft touch," and there is no doubt that Ellie and my sons regard Sasha as "spoiled" by me.

3

❖ THE PARK ❖

Part of the covenant between man and a husky should be a serious commitment to exercise. These dogs need activity like running flat-out, and if they get it, they are much easier to deal with the rest of the time. As with all dogs, they are capable of hours of quiet time, but during even quiet time, Sasha rarely is deeply asleep. If someone stirs, her eyes are instantly open. If she does not get a walk, or much better, a run or a climb, she will begin to negotiate by staring intently at the improvident one; if that doesn't work, she will gradually escalate to vocalizing in a manner unique to these wolf-dogs, something between a bark and a howl, expressive and varied. If you respond with a brief comment, she will continue what she regards as her argument as long as you continue to respond.

Fortunately for Sasha and the City of Seattle, there was once upon a time a naval air base on Lake Washington, not far from downtown. It achieved some degree of fame as a refueling site for an aerial circumnavigation of the world. Its concrete runways were short, limited by the dimensions of the Sand Point peninsula, but adequate for propeller aircraft. By the time jets became standard on military aircraft, the area around Sand Point was heavily developed, and expansion of the runways into Lake Washington was not politically feasible. The fate of the airport was sealed by the crash of a military jet north of the airport into an occupied house resulting in two deaths. Although the Navy continued various facilities at the site after that, they abandoned its use as an air field.

The concrete runways were immensely attractive to private pilots in the area and they organized an intense campaign to have Sand Point turned over to civilian aviation. But by this time, the number of residents who would be adversely affected by the noise was far greater than the number of private plane owners. Still, the issue remained in doubt until Washington's venerable and effective Senator Magnuson quietly pushed through legislation that set aside a small part of Sand Point for an installation of the National Oceanographic and Atmospheric Administration, in addition to the continuing non-aviation functions of the Naval Air Command, and the remaining land was deeded back to the city. After briefly testing the political winds, the city officials tore out the concrete runways, developed a small part of the land by building boat launches and picnic areas, and left the remaining many acres in an undeveloped state, except for some graveled paths.

The undeveloped part of Sand Point is a world of meadows, Scot's broom, and blackberry bushes for exploring, and some man-made mounds that are perfect for king-of-the-mountain games, or in Sasha's case, queen-of-the-mountain. During the spring rains, there are small ponds for cooling feet and for scooping up water for drinking on the dead run. There are redwing blackbirds, goldfinches, robins, California quail, owls, hawks, ducks, Canada geese, and even an occasional bald eagle. There are coyotes by several reports and small beasties that burrow in the ground, whose burrows stimulate intense digging by Sasha.

Sasha's digging at the park is not always aimed at withdrawals, and frequently leads to deposits—at least temporarily. Ellie rewards her with dog cookies for returning on command and other heroic achievements and sometimes Sasha decides on her own that she deserves a reward. But she is not always ready to eat the reward—then she finds a soft spot in the ground and excavates a shallow receptacle for her morsel and covers it with dirt nudged into place by her nose.

Unlike the squirrels who seem to have great difficulty remembering where their nuts have been deposited, Sasha invariably digs up her treasure the next day, even if she isn't actually ready to eat it. If she isn't hungry, she will select a new bank for the redeposit. Occasionally, the deposit may not be strictly edible. If she finds a leather glove, she "kills" it by vigorous shaking, and buries it until the next day. She will repeat that process daily, sometimes for weeks.

The population of visitors to the "outback" is ever-changing, but still familiar. Many are regulars, who show up each day at the same time, but other dogs are less fortunate and only come on the weekend. Sasha is in the privileged class, thanks to Ellie. The people in the outback, just as the dogs, vary in gregariousness, ranging from those who assiduously avoid any contact, to those who are oblivious of others' desire for privacy.

Sasha seems finely attuned to these attitudes; she senses un-friendly "vibes" from either dog or owner, and simply ignores their existence. However, she has many admirers, two- and four-footed. For her human friends, her greeting is quite specific, with eye contact, a brief tail-wag and softening of her ears, and an un-mistakable smile. What is not anticipated by most people is her dislike of being petted.

From the earliest puppy days Sasha has shown a distaste for having her head petted, or her ears scratched. It is as though she regards that as beneath her status as a Siberian-American princess. Whatever the reason, this distaste is in contrast to her obvious af-fection for the two of us and for many of her friends.

It is somewhat embarrassing to have her pull back from a friendly hand, as though afraid of being struck, although there is never any cringing, characteristic of abused animals. Her new ad-mirers are frustrated by such an adorable-looking pup who wants no physical contact. The only time she asks for petting is when the "other kids are having some," particularly Tioga and Nootka—then she will shoulder in for her share, looking just a little embar-rassed. However, her status as a princess permits her to nose-kiss, but even then with discretion: she touches only the very tip of your nose if you bend down, and it is never a sloppy, wet kiss.

Although Sasha is gregarious, she has definite favorite dogs at the park, usually *lupus*-types. These animals, like members of a wolf pack, know how to play with simulated combat that sounds serious, but with enthusiastic good humor, and they continue to enjoy these games long after puppyhood.

Occasionally, a newcomer has to establish his or her dominance, and there is a brief, earnest confrontation. Although Sasha has a remarkable tolerance for pain, she also firmly believes in the quickest possible surrender if an opponent seeks dominance. The pack ethic of huskies requires the cessation of hostilities at once when surrender is tendered, and Sasha has never been hung-up on dominance. A genuine assault leads to loud, prophylactic screams, calculated to embarrass the aggressor. Sasha doesn't appear cowed, but simply looks offended that anyone would want to spoil a good "wrassle."

Of course, Sasha disdains the priorities of other breeds, just as they fail to appreciate hers. She watches the retrievers endlessly chase sticks and balls and is interested only in chasing the retriever. She developed her swimming skills by chasing a golden Labrador chasing a stick thrown into the lake; Sasha swam behind, biting his tail and rear feet. The Lab almost foundered trying to swim and growl while holding onto the stick.

Sasha initially learned to swim on a hot day when she was about six months old. She was wading back and forth, cooling off, but not venturing into deeper water. A charming Romanian gentleman was swimming nearby and volunteered to teach Sasha how to swim. Ellie, unsympathetic to harsh "swim or sink" training methods, politely declined. However, as she described it, he was the most persuasive man she had ever opposed, and he was very persistent. Finally persuaded, Ellie agreed to his plan to gently hold her (Sasha, that is) and wade out a few feet and release her. Sasha swam quite effectively back to shore, and just as Ellie had feared, ran off. Fortunately, he was a man of his word, and he helped Ellie catch the wily wolf-pup.

The small, wild animals in the park, although of great interest to Sasha, are rarely affected by her for the simple reason that there is enough traffic by potential predators to teach the survivors caution. In addition, animals that burrow know enough to have

Sasha hunting in the "outback" of Magnuson Park. She is soaring, preparing to pounce down and flush any mice out of hiding. (Photo by Karl Guntheroth).

more than one exit. These safeguards permit us to watch and admire as she performs ancient rituals of the hunt. She has excellent balance and strength which enables her to stand quietly in the tall grass, on her hind feet, in the manner of a relative, the bear. When she runs in the grass, she bounds high and soars like a deer looking for action. These graceful runs end with a "diving-board bounce," when all her feet come down close together, to scare a hiding mouse into jumping, revealing its location. I had never seen this pounce before except in National Geographic shows of hunting wolves or coyotes, whose diet consists of *many* mice.

Shortly after she learned to swim Sasha encountered another intended victim, a mallard duck. The mallard was alone, paddling close to the shore. Sasha subtly—she thought—began silently swimming toward the duck. The mallard was not really alarmed, and taunted Sasha with loud quacks and swam only fast enough to maintain the separation between them, and with little perceptible effort. Sasha seemed encouraged by the fact that the duck didn't fly away, and diligently pursued the prey.

What she did not notice was that the duck was swimming farther and farther away from shore. Ellie soon became alarmed, since it was only the second or third time Sasha had been swimming, and she looked anxiously for a fisherman with a boat or *any* boat to rescue her pup. Happily, Sasha's endurance was excellent, even if her speed as a swimmer was not, and she calmly swam back after half an hour, with unshaken confidence.

Sasha continues to swim, but according to how warm it is. During the winter, she rarely wades in the lake, but after a vigorous chase with a friend, may flop down in an icy puddle for a kind of Scandinavian treat. But in hot weather, particularly if she has been running hard, she will swim out and literally do laps, back and forth. She does not like hot weather, but her inventiveness allows her to cope with it quite well.

4

❖ SASHA'S EARLY CLIMBS ❖

One of the considerations in adopting Sasha was that I spent many days and weekends climbing and skiing in the Cascades and Olympic Mountains. Ellie shares my enthusiasm for skiing—at least downhill skiing on packed slopes—but not for climbing, as opposed to modest hikes. Her attitude toward my climbing may be summarized as, "If you don't object to my not climbing with you, I won't object to your climbing without me."

Nevertheless, during the unusual Seattle summer with persistent good weather, Ellie sometimes is less tolerant of my frequent absences, and both of us thought that a lively pup might be good company for her. (The downside was that Ellie would have to babysit the pup.)

Since I had almost never climbed with our dogs Tigger and Sigi from earlier years, this seemed like a reasonable scenario. Sasha's first mountain outing did nothing to change the plan of Sasha as Ellie's companion.

Mount Si. A ride home, please?

Sasha was only 14 weeks old. It was a cool, cloudy day in early April, with drizzle—in short, a typical Seattle day. Although it was Saturday, my climbing buddy Ed had to work overtime at Boeing. It was raining in the mountain passes, and persuading Ellie to ski in the rain would have been grounds for divorce. Climbing Mount Si seemed like a reasonable way to get some exercise.

For spring climbing, Mount Si is a good bet since it is only a 45 minute drive from Seattle, and its base is a mere 700 feet above sea level, guaranteeing access almost all year. The summit is over 4000 feet; consequently there is usually snow in April on the northeast side of the summit block, affectionately known as "the haystack." But most of the 3000 feet up to the meadow at the base of the haystack is hiked on a four mile trail.

I have climbed Mount Si probably 60 times. But on this occasion, I thought I would try the legs and stamina of our little wolf-dog. Ellie, as a veteran mother-figure, argued that Sasha might get lost, or stolen because she was so attractive!

I reassured her with Phil's claim that Ulu could always find her way without ever getting lost, even when he couldn't actually see her. If that phrase is carefully analyzed, it suggests that Ulu didn't ever acknowledge being lost but there might be times when Phil didn't know where she was. But being a father-type, and a Leo, I put aside Ellie's concerns and loaded up my Celica hatchback with Sasha and my climbing boots.

Sasha was a little anxious, since she had not been confined to a car for more than the 15 minutes required to go to the park. However, she finally settled down on the back seat. When we got to the parking lot on the east side of Si, I folded my seat forward and she jumped out. Unfortunately, her right dew claw caught firmly in the seat lever, and her momentum carried her out of the car, minus the claw. She uttered one loud scream and spun around to inspect her injury. Her foot bled briskly as I tried to comfort her. I reluctantly decided that she would not want to go anywhere but home, and I was trying to coax her back into the car, when she simply trotted off up the trail. I decided that I had better put on my boots and join her.

In spite of the weather, there were at least 50 cars in the lot, and probably a hundred climbers on the trail, and at least 15 dogs—no cats—to my estimate. The trail is steep, and relentlessly so, but not for Sasha. After we had gone a couple of miles, I realized that I had not seen her for some minutes—the last I had seen of her was heading off the trail, straight up the hill, toward the next switchback.

At some point, she apparently decided that I was lost, and cut back down to find me. By that time I had passed the point of her intersection, still going uphill. As I have found on several occasions since then, Sasha's incredible ability to track my scent does not include the ability to determine whether I was going up or down the trail. On this occasion, she followed my tracks back to the car. Since I wasn't sure where she was, I started down, but at least 15 minutes behind her. Furthermore, I could not go nearly so fast as she, even with her injury.

As I strode down the trail, I would inquire of those pilgrims coming up whether they had seen a husky puppy. Fortunately, Sasha is memorable to most people, and I determined that she was indeed heading back down.

Walking as rapidly as I could I was filled with dread, thinking of what I would say to Ellie, who had warned of all this. To say that Sasha was not bonded to me at that point was to seriously understate the case. I was sure she would take off with anyone with food, or even an open car door. In fact, just as I walked into the parking lot, she was entering a hiker's car, much to his surprise.

It was a very happy reunion, as far as I was concerned—but for Sasha, with whom she would leave the dance was a question of little importance.

The first summit.

I no longer trusted Sasha in the mountains, and the rest of that first summer she stayed home with Ellie while Ed and I climbed a variety of peaks in the Cascades and Olympics. The autumn that year was astonishingly warm and sunny, and in late October, Ellie agreed to a hike up to Eagle Lake. She and Sasha would explore around the lake while I climbed nearby Townsend Mountain.

The initial half mile between the lake and the mountainside was flat but difficult because of thick brush and downed trees, but soon I was out of the trees, onto a mostly treeless slope of boulder fields and meadows of grass and heather. I could then see the lake shore and finally located Ellie, but no Sasha.

29

The reason was soon obvious as she emerged from the trees not far from me, having run most of the way from the lake. She was panting, and clearly hot. She soon demonstrated her strategy for the remainder of the climb, trotting between the few trees, flopping down in the shade, and waiting for dad.

She also showed her distaste for boulder fields by waiting at the bottom of them, visually plotting my course through them, and then circumnavigating them on the grass. With her energy, it didn't matter if she had to go a longer distance, it was how she got there. This ability to observe direction and speed to intercept her target is probably an inherited skill, essential for a successful hunt in her ancestors' lives.

As we neared the summit of the long ridge, she picked up her pace, and summitted several minutes before me. As has become her custom, she looked down at her slower human companion with what seemed to be a smirk.

On the descent, Sasha stuck relatively close to me as we went back to the lake. Ellie had already started down, thinking she would not have to hurry. The lower we got on the trail, the fresher

A young Sasha being held by Karl, with her ears down, indicating displeasure in this position. They are flanked by Sten on the left, and Kurt on the right.

was Ellie's scent, and finally Sasha took off. Needless to say, Ellie was surprised to be overtaken by a solitary and enthusiastic Princess, several minutes before I caught up with them.

The Pilchuck sacrifice.

That glorious October day on Townsend was the last good weekend of that year, as it turned out. We turned to downhill skiing, until a Sunday in early January, when Ed and I thought we would introduce Sasha to her heritage of snow.

Although Seattle is literally surrounded by mountains, it snows only once or twice a year at sea level, and that first year of Sasha's life, it had not snowed at all. It was literally her first birthday when we drove up to Mount Pilchuck, a respectable peak relatively close to Puget Sound, easily seen from Interstate 5. It had been a ski area for some years, but finally closed because it was too challenging for most skiers. (Ed and I loved it, but even we had reservations about some aspects, including the wetness of the snow, and the fact that, as the first peak off the ocean, it tended to collect an inordinate amount of bad weather.)

This Sunday was no exception for weather, with sleet and snow driven by strong winds as we pulled into the abandoned parking lot. The snow level began only 50 feet above the parking lot. Sasha seemed blasé about her first snow. She calmly walked onto it, and seemed to recognize it as an old acquaintance—there was no barking or rolling in it, just a business-like trotting ahead, maintaining her lead position.

When the snow got deeper and she could not walk in the usual way, she spontaneously began to porpoise, leaping forward on all four feet. When temporarily exhausted, she would simply rest at the end of the forward leap, cooling her belly, before resuming her vigorous locomotion. She frequently had to wait for us, and would search out a small hump, and lie down facing back toward her slow bipeds, who were wishing they had 4-wheel drive, or at least had brought their snowshoes.

The final approach to the summit was steep and the trail was lost under four feet of snow, and Sasha occasionally whined very softly, inquiring if we really thought this was a reasonable thing to be doing, in the teeth of a gale. Undaunted, the humans pushed on toward the summit with its abandoned lookout cabin, used for fire watches until 1956. The cabin was not difficult to find in the whiteout, since it is on the very edge of a precipice, and the approach simply hugged the rim. Ed and I had no problem getting on to the platform that runs around the outside of most lookouts, but there were no stairs, only a ladder constructed of two-by-fours. Sasha was puzzled, and a little anxious. I made a major mistake by lifting her and placing her onto the platform. I should have anticipated her reaction, because she regarded being picked up as an act of extreme humiliation.

An otherwise favorite picture of ours is of Sasha in the arms of our son Karl, her ears down, a very unusual position for her, indicating severe displeasure.

Adding to the indignity of being picked up, the storm and the threatening position of the cabin, almost overhanging the precipice, convinced her that things were not right. Sasha concluded that we had brought her up there to make a living sacrifice to the mountain gods. To my horror, she immediately flung herself off the platform; fortunately, she took time to choose the side away from the cliff. There followed the usual apologies and attempts to pet her, which were quite futile; she was uncompromising in her paranoia.

Ed and I gave up, and went into the shelter that was closed on three sides, and dug our lunches out of our packs. Meanwhile, the storm raged outside, and Sasha smelled food, always of intense interest. She investigated the cabin perimeter systematically and discovered a snow drift on the side opposite the ladder, and was quickly in our faces, inquiring about *her* lunch. She got it, and a fair part of ours.

She has not forgotten that experience to this day. She shows the same paranoia for any summit with very limited space.

Evergreen Mountain and the porcupine.
By May, it was apparent that Sasha really enjoyed snow, and in a couple of outings she had demonstrated her sure-footed skills, with little fear of heights, as long as she was on her *own* four feet. With the end of the skiing season, and opening of some of the log-

ging roads, we drove past Jack Pass, and left the car when the snow became deep.

We started hiking the road toward the trailhead to Evergreen Mountain. After a quarter of a mile, Sasha came running silently from behind us on the road, unusual for this alpha-dog who likes to be in the lead.

When she caught up, she seemed quite agitated, and buried her face in the snow, and appeared to be trying to rub off something from her muzzle. Sasha had tasted a porcupine! There were 15 to 20 quills in her nose and lips. She let me remove one of the slippery quills, but then backed away.

We returned to the car, and armed with pliers, I again tried to remove them. She held still for two, which is surprising in retrospect. But then she trotted purposefully away down the logging road toward Seattle, indicating that she wanted no more of that treatment. We finally convinced her to get into the car and she rode back to Seattle with her chin held carefully off the seat, to avoid driving the diabolical quills in farther.

Finally home, Sasha silently crept under my bureau, a favorite hiding place, with drooping ears and tail. Ellie took her to the vet, grumbling only a little about how come *she* got the duty and I had the fun. The veterinarian had worked in eastern Washington and was an old pro about quills, in spite of her apparent youth. She used a rapidly acting general anesthetic, cut off the tips of the quills, which deflates the little devils, and removed them one by one. After about an hour, and an intravenous dose of a drug that counteracted the anesthetic, Sasha was her usual bright-eyed self.

Sasha has encountered three more porcupines in her climbing career, and from one she got a single quill from his tail, barely into her muzzle. She barked persistently to us, asking us to come destroy the monster; this was the only time she has ever barked in the mountains, except for her first encounter with a dog-eating horse.

Sasha recovered without a mark from the quills. Although they fester in wild animals who don't have friendly vets, due to a foreign body reaction intrinsic in all animals, the quills are actually sterile. It was only a couple of weeks before she was out in the mountains again.

The moat on Eagle Rock.

Ed and I had selected a couple of peaks for this spring outing, Flapjack Point and Eagle Rock, which were approached from a logging road that comes within a mile or two of Eagle Lake. On this sunny but cool day in May the road was drivable to just past Eagle Creek.

The route from there was entirely cross-country; that is, there was no trail. The first half mile was across a clear-cut that had never been replanted, and was full of downed trees that were not judged profitable for hauling. Sasha did much better than we in this section, since she could crawl under many of the logs, and for others, she demonstrated one of her cat-like skills by leaping gracefully onto a log, and running down its length, stopping long enough to be admired, and exiting with another sure-footed leap.

Within an hour, we had reached the snow, which was firm enough that it compressed only an inch or less with our Vibram soles, which improved our travel time through the gap and up the long ridge to Flapjack.

We reached the summit in one and a half hours from the car, and had a snack. As we headed back down the ridge, we began a leftward traverse in order to reach the base of the second peak. The hillside was steep, and the snow hardened, but Sasha demonstrated the advantage of four feet equipped with built-in crampons (her claws).

Examining her footprints revealed that she was spreading her toes and digging in with her claws with each step; occasionally, there would be a smear from a brief slide, ending in a particularly deep claw print where she had "self arrested."

The last 500 feet of the summit were also snow covered, except for a 30 foot section in the middle that was more vertical. This was the steepest terrain that Sasha had so far encountered, but she stayed in the lead and wound her way through some small trees and ledges to the snow above, and then distanced herself from the slow-pokes. She reached the summit at least 15 minutes before us, thoroughly exploring the area, but frequently coming back to peer over the edge to confirm that our destination was the same as hers.

Dad sharing a summit lunch. (Photo by Ed Emery).

Although Sasha at home is fed only once a day in the evening, she was much hungrier on these climbs, and to protect my own lunch, I began to carry a lunch for her. Even so, she pretended that she was starving, and got as close to my sandwich as she could manage, which was very close. Although Ellie was firmly set against feeding dogs at the table, there was no table on the mountain, and Sasha was quick to exploit the difference.

All of the dogs I have known seem convinced that if you sat on the ground that you were volunteering for a face-to-face encounter with them, which included a certain amount of tasting. Sasha was no exception, except that when food was nearby, the intensity of the encounter was greatly enhanced, but with remarkable gentleness.

Even Ed, who professed not to like dogs, began to share his lunch with this seductive wolf-dog. Of course, he had never really known a person such as Sasha, and he rationalized that his growing attachment to her was because she had many cat-like features, such as independence, "climbing" trees, and an agility unknown to most dogs.

The south side of the summit was snow-free, with grass and avalanche lilies creating a pleasant place to eat and to lie in the sun, while Sasha explored, proving the superiority of her strength and energy over these tired humans. Soon, however, a few clouds drifted over, and the instant cooling caused us to reconsider the idle life and start back toward the car.

Running downhill in snow is one of life's sweetest experiences to Sasha; the look on her face appears to be pure pleasure. She uses a canine form of the climber's plunge step, which is performed by humans with a stiff-legged plant of the heel during a steep descent in snow. Sasha keeps her fully extended front legs together to break the snow to slow her descent. But if the snow is not too steep, she seems to slide on the bottom of her rear legs, while rapidly moving her front ones. Consequently, the first 500 feet of the descent were executed enthusiastically by the wolf-pup.

When she got to the more vertical part, she explored cautiously and then waited for us. We tried the route we had ascended, but some snow had slabbed off, leaving a steep bit of sloping, wet rock which neither Sasha nor her followers were willing to trust, since it was at the top of the section which could have led to a 30 foot fall.

After some exploring, Ed and I chose a series of small ledges that ended at a moat at the bottom of the steep section. The moat was only two or three feet wide, and once over it, there was a long section of not-so-steep snow ending in a safe run-out that gradually leveled off. Sasha descended the ledges bravely enough, inventing a technique that we envied; she lowered her weight onto her flexed rear legs, balanced herself, and then carefully placed her front feet on the lower ledge one at a time. If the front feet slipped, she had enough strength and balance to recover her position on the upper ledge. The moat, however, was something else! She had never been required to jump a hungry mouth that had ugly rocks in its stomach, and she began to vocalize her concerns.

We backtracked several times to demonstrate the technique of jumping the moat, but she remained unconvinced. We finally descended just out of sight, ignoring her tragic howls, and waited. It was less than a minute before she passed us—she would not stop to collect our praise and affection, ignoring those who had cruelly abandoned her. By the time we reached the gap she had forgiven us, but her skills in descending were permanently enhanced.

Palmer Mountain and the pathfinder.

Only two months had passed when Sasha again got to climb
with me, on a peak close to Skykomish. Ed concluded that the
weather was unsuited for climbing—he was right—and just Sasha
and I set out to find a logging road off Money Creek. The first
branch was no problem, but finding the second road required careful odometer readings and frequent exploration on foot to identify
the remnants of a road to an abandoned quarry. The directions in
Beckey's guide (officially the *Cascade Alpine Guide*) were char-
acteristically brief and ambiguous.

Congratulating myself on reaching the quarry (not mentioned
in the guide) at the end of the road, I looked for a reasonable way
around the quarry to attain the east ridge, while Sasha checked out
a small pond. I chose to ascend a ridge just south of the quarry, a
steep and gravelly climb ending in a two foot wide ledge that traversed the entire headwall formed by the excavation.

Although there was a drop off the ledge of at least 200 feet,
the ledge did not bother Sasha, and we were soon climbing up the
main east ridge. We hiked in a cool drizzle, with very limited visibility. However, white-out conditions are not much of a problem
going *up* a mountain as long as there is only one true summit; you
keep going up until there isn't anymore "up!"

The summit block finally loomed out of the fog, and it was
more exciting than I had anticipated from inspection of the contour
map, which had altitude intervals of 80 feet (a 50 foot cliff would
appear to be a simple stroll to the summit). For Palmer Mountain
the summit block was anything but a walk-up. After seeing the
first vertical step, it was obvious that Sasha would not be able to
make the actual summit, so I put her on "stay," and climbed up as
rapidly as I could manage.

As befits a husky described by Lorenz, "stay" is quite a flex-
ible concept to Sasha. Although she stayed reasonably close to the
spot from which I ascended, she never gave up exploring for an
alternate route for an ambitious four-legged climber. On this bleak
day she did not find another route, but within 15 minutes, I was back
to her and my pack. We had our lunches hunkered down below
the ridge, with our backs to the wind, as the mist swirled around

37

us, hiding anything and everything from view except each other.

I confess that I did not look forward to the descent, given the weather and poor visibility, but the choices were quite limited. We started off bravely enough, but in less than ten minutes I came across a patch of snow that resembled the only patch we had encountered on the way up. The initial reassurance of being on track quickly gave way to wonder: there were tracks on the patch, as there should be, but they were going in the direction we were then heading. I should have noticed that Sasha was not well out in front as is her custom when she is confident that we are on the right vector. Instead, she was close by me, looking a little puzzled, as was I!

As usual in situations that are unacceptable, I rationalized that the snow patch was a different one, and that the tracks going in the "wrong" direction must have been left by someone else that same day. Of course, the chances that there were two solitary climbers crazy enough to be climbing in that weather on a mountain that probably hadn't been climbed all that year, let alone that day, was vanishingly small, but I was reluctant to concede that I was turned around a full 180 degrees.

The top of the mountain was a plateau with a summit block, so there was little gain or loss in altitude as I strode ahead through the whiteout. When the summit block suddenly loomed up again in the fog, my confidence vanished. I got out the compass, and carefully started back toward the east ridge, and the snow patch.

This time, the tracks made sense, and I lined up the compass and the map and started down. For the first time since lunch, Sasha realized that we were going home, and the change in her attitude was striking; her tail was arched over her back, her ears were up, and she walked purposefully, high on her toes. It was also obvious that she was following our scent.

The route finding problems were not over, however. First, it was difficult to see Sasha much of the time, and I frequently had to whistle her back. To my relief, she sensed that she was doing something important and always returned to my side if I continued to whistle. I could then adjust my route toward where she had appeared. The second problem for me was that of picking the correct downhill branch of each junction with the ridge we were on, quite a different proposition from that of going up, when there was no ambiguity. Frequently, true east was exactly between the two candidate branch ridges, and Sasha had to decide for us which was the correct one.

Meanwhile, it was getting darker and the drizzle had turned into a steady rain. I had put on my Gore-tex parka near the summit, but as I well knew, this fabric works well for yuppies who are out running for 30 minutes, and if you continue to be in the rain for longer than that, you should count on being wet. (In spite of that knowledge, there isn't anything better—the truly waterproof parkas cause as much wetness from sweat!)

The disagreeable thought of having to spend a night on this mountain, with thoroughly wet clothes and a hungry pup kept me going down as fast as I could without sliding on the wet evergreen needles. Although I cannot say that *any* of the ridge was truly familiar to me, I finally sensed that I had never seen the specific terrain I was on.

It dawned on me that if I missed the narrow ledge back to the other side of the quarry, I would completely miss the road which came into the quarry from the other side, and really be stuck with a night out. I turned around and reluctantly climbed back uphill, with complaining legs. After gaining a couple of hundred feet, I sensed that I had again missed the ledge. My confidence in my pathfinding was shaken, but I once more descended.

During this period of uncertainty, Sasha looked puzzled, and stayed close to my side, a position that means she is following me, not leading. This time down, Sasha abruptly trotted ahead and to the right, stopped, and looked over her shoulder in a way that said rather plainly, "Is *this* what you are looking for?" Well, it was the elusive ledge and Sasha received elaborate and enthusiastic praise. Now, she had become a trusted ally in the struggle with the uncaring mountains.

5

❖ FOOD ❖

Gifted athletes possess an uncommon ability to concentrate on every aspect of their performance. Sasha's general alertness seems to be more constant than any other dog I have known and her concentration on food is particularly intense.

This trait may have been crucial to survival of the breed over the centuries in their native harsh and unforgiving milieu. Perhaps their present independence and lack of total submission may stem from the uncomfortable fact that dogs *are* edible, so that not only did Siberian huskies have to fend for themselves for their own food, they may have had to protect themselves from becoming the prey.

(I do not know that the Siberian Eskimo ate dog meat during famine times, but the Norwegian explorers under Amundsen did during their race to the South Pole. The English under Scott refused to indulge in the "unchristian" eating of even horse meat, which contributed both to their failure to be first to the pole and to their deaths.)

In short, alertness in general and toward food specifically is a strategy for survival of the breed, and Sasha demonstrates the trait to perfection.

Sasha is, plainly put, untrustworthy with food. This is particularly striking if you have owned a shepherd or similar breed. My first dog as a child was part-Airedale, who was so obedient that a morsel of food dropped on the ground was not touched until specific permission was given. (Pat was not above stealing food from neighbor children, whom he regarded as having no claim superior to his, particularly if they were in his yard.)

As a pup, Sasha's foraging was aided by her ability to rise quietly on her rear legs and directly inspect the table and kitchen counter. Needless to say, a box of chocolates left on the floor under the Christmas tree would pose little problem, either physically or morally. As she has matured, there are fewer predations, perhaps because we are more on guard, and perhaps because she has developed more of a conscience.

Sasha's attitude toward theft and punishment is reminiscent of some human behavior, namely, an acceptance of punishment if the particular temptation is sufficient. It then becomes an obvious transaction. Once, when Ellie had an early evening counsellor's meeting, I was warming up a bowl of stew in the microwave oven. I had just sliced a large piece of French bread, and had left it on my plate, thickly buttered. I became aware of a scrambling noise from the dining room, a certain sign of mischief. When Sasha wants attention, she will steal something relatively innocuous, such as a paper towel, and then scramble out of reach under a couch or bureau, and shred it with her teeth.

On this evening, it was quickly obvious that she was not playing, but had stolen the piece of bread. The exceptional behavior this evening was that she left her rear end out from under the sideboard, accessible to manual swatting, which was accompanied by severe statements about her ancestry. Her head *was* protected, which left her free to consume the entire piece. She had deliberately contracted for the piece of buttered bread to be paid for with a spanking.

The fact that the stolen bread was buttered was not insignificant. On occasion she has stolen and eaten an entire quarter-pound of butter or margarine. I presume that in the arctic, fat with its double load of calories per gram is especially attractive. I don't know whether her addiction to chocolate is based on its fat content, but there is *no* question that Sasha would kill for it.

Sasha's illustrious veterinarian, Dr. Canfield, is strong in his opposition to chocolate for dogs, reporting that seizures and even death can result from an "overdose" and I rarely exceed three M&Ms (with peanuts) as her bedtime ritual. On the other hand, when she consumed two and a half pounds of stolen chocolates one Christmas Eve, she was not the least worse for wear. (They were white chocolate, which may have made a difference.)

After all sweets, to protect her teeth, I have conscientiously provided her with a canine "toothbrush," a hard dog biscuit.

Her other favorite treat also has a high oil content—the cat's "veterinary special" food. Like many neutered male cats, several years of dry cat chow left Snidely with bladder stones, an extremely unpleasant condition. The special food contains oil to increase the calories and reduce the residual solids from bone meal. Snidely was fed this twice a day, and Sasha can hear the sound of pellets dropping into the cat's dish from several rooms away. She requests, and gets, a half-dozen of these little pellets each morning, even after Snidely's passing.

Dinner time at our house is a special time for me, the hour when I feel most lonesome if I am away for long climbs, or on business. This special feeling is due to Ellie's efforts over the 40 years of our marriage. It is a time for a cocktail and snacks of some sort, frequently nuts, or when my weight permits, Brie and Triscuits. It goes without saying that Sasha approves of the predinner social time, and expects something different from her customary evening meal of Purina dog chow spiked with some canned dog food.

Her appetizer currently consists of two slices of brick cheese, broken into small bits to make them last while we have ours. She frequently waits to eat her dog food until she finds out what special treats we are having. If she finally is told "no more," she reluctantly—but promptly—turns to her regular food.

Unless she is unusually hungry, she will attempt to shame us by bringing out to the dining room a single dried pellet, which she spits out forcefully, pounces on it, and tosses it over her back. After we have had an opportunity to fully grasp the unfairness of our behavior, she reluctantly consumes the pellet with obvious sarcasm.

42

Sasha is an artful beggar. Although Ellie is convinced that permitting begging at the table is reprehensible, my intransigence has weakened her resolve somewhat, since no one wants to be the "heavy" all of the time. We have reached a compromise of sorts: no matter how much Sasha pleads, she is rarely fed until the end of our meal. Consequently, during most meals she does not beg, although she usually lies under our feet.

It is not evident to me what tips her off to the presence of bones on our plates, but she invariably knows. Her sense of justice asserts her right to these, and she does not wait for the meal to end to argue her case for bones.

Sasha exhibits two basic techniques in her quest for bones and other morsels. The first is an intense stare focused on the one with the bone, a stare which we call "the death stare," described by Barry Lopez in his book, *Of Wolves and Men*.

If you reach over to pat her head while she is in this mode, she quickly pulls her head away with a reproachful look that seems to say "Don't *touch* me."

Her more recent technique is infinitely more successful: head on lap, with escalating pressure, and snuggling increasingly closer, and finally, rolling the head and eyes upward with her best effort at appearing tragic. If no response is forthcoming, her final effort is to rest one paw on my knee.

When we have ice cream for dessert Sasha gets to lick the spoon and the nearly empty carton. From her place beneath the table, she recognizes the sound of the freezer compartment being opened, and immediately trots to the kitchen. Afterwards, and in fact, after any meal that meets her approval, she heads for the family room rug, and thoroughly rubs her muzzle as though the rug were a napkin.

Manipulation is not a one-way street; we use it on her as well. When we had to leave Sasha alone, before we installed a pet door, we would leave her on the outside deck which connects by stairs to a small, fenced enclosure. To entice her out onto the deck, we always gave her a doggie biscuit, telling her that "Sasha can't go." This Pavlovian technique worked so well that when she observes us dressing to go out, she runs down stairs before us and eagerly waits at the door to the deck, confident of the treat. (Of course, with a pet door, she immediately returns indoors after she scarfs down the biscuit, but she does not seem sad to see us go.) In short, another mutually satisfactory transaction occurs between us.

Another of Sasha's talents that is applied in her diligent quest for food is her precise internal clock. My bedtime snack of M&Ms comes at the end of my work day in my study, and since I am a creature of habit, that occurs regularly at 10:30pm. At 10:25, give or take five minutes, Sasha silently rises from her rest and walks over to my desk and sits at attention, waiting for her M&Ms. Unlike our clocks and watches, Sasha does not recognize daylight saving time, and this causes difficulty for a while after the biannual resetting. She seems indignant when I tell her it isn't time yet for her treat.

Although I was convinced that Sasha had an appetite control that allowed her to eat anything she wanted and when she wanted it, this conviction finally was eroded by her increasingly Rubenesque curves. For a while, I blamed it on her winter fur, and we were lulled by earlier weighing episodes that confirmed she still was only 50 pounds.

Of course, weighing her was not a particularly pleasant matter. She immediately sensed evil when approached with sweet talk, like a child warned about strangers with candy. If possible she would scramble under something. Eventually she would submit to being picked up, with all of the histrionics of a Camille about to die. Walking with her tense body in my arms, climbing onto the small bathroom scale, and maneuvering to see the read-out actually justifies her concern for her safety; I certainly worry about *my* safety. Finally, we reach a brief equilibrium, and we subtract my weight from the gross weight.

It had been quite a while since we had gone through this procedure; the scales told the awful truth, that Sasha had gained *eight* pounds. We thought that we had made an error, but not so!

We knew it wouldn't be easy, but our love was up to the difficult task. Sasha went on a diet. We decided to only reduce the size of every serving, rather than eliminating any of her favorites. Our dedication was bolstered by the fact that she had grown less active during her obesity, something we had attributed to "maturation," and we were encouraged as she gradually lost the entire eight pounds. Oddly enough, she tolerated her diet then, and now, with surprising equanimity, all things considered.

Maintaining her svelte condition has been made easier by a thoughtful memorial gift to Sasha's vet, a walk-on scale for pets, which is available any day without an appointment. Sasha has figured out the routine, and now simply trots over and stands quietly on the scale. Of course, as with all of us, continuing vigilance is necessary against the enemy of obesity.

6

❖ TIOGA, NOOTKA and ❖ SKIING

When Sasha was a year and a half old, middle son Karl and his wife Katie adopted two malamute puppies, a boy they named Tioga, and a girl, Nootka. Although the Alaskan huskies closely resemble the Siberian huskies, there are some important differences, such as size: the Alaskan variety are about twice the size of their Siberian relatives (see photo on facing page).

Secondly, their temperament is more like the traditional *Canis aureus*, a result of cross-breeding. In the case of Tioga and Nootka, there was somewhat more of the *lupus* because the father was a thoroughbred Samoyed. These two dogs are similar in height but Tioga weighs about 20 pounds more. The male is a striking cream color; the female has a white face, but her body is a mixture of contrasting shades of brown. Both of them have long, silky hair. Tioga has always had erect ears, like Sasha, but for years Nootka rarely was able to get more than one ear up at a time, creating a charming, vulnerable look. Now, however, her ears stand erect.

As for personality, the two were remarkably different, particularly in the first year. Tioga was a laid back dude, so quiet that I worried that he had some undiagnosed ailment. Nootka demonstrated a much higher energy level from the first, and bonded quickly to the high-octane "Aunt Sasha."

Sasha in the park with her "niece and nephew," Tioga on her right and Nootka on her left. These malamutes are brother and sister, and weigh twice as much as Sasha. Ellie is holding the leashes.

Tioga was always content to use his bulk, which is considerable, to end arguments. I have never known him to bare his teeth except in play. Nootka, on the other hand, has never met another dog she liked, except for her brother and Sasha. Even on a leash, she consistently started fights with other dogs, particularly males. I have only seen her lose one fight, and that clearly made her resolved to try again and again until she finally was able to take *him* down. But with Sasha and her brother, and happily, all humans, she is the most affectionate dog known to me, and more recently, she has mellowed out with other dogs to some extent.

From the very beginning, Aunt Sasha loved these two pups. She was spayed, but had a patently maternal approach to them, who were only three months old, while Sasha was all of 18 months. Sasha immediately set about training them how to play, and play they did! Tioga tired more quickly for the first year, and tended to back off and watch; later, his stamina equalled and even surpassed his sister's, but he never has caught up to Sasha, due to fewer opportunities for anything but short walks.

The play of these three is a delight to watch. By six months of age the malamutes were bigger than the Siberian, but that never phased Sasha, as long as they were in the play mode. (On the rare occasion when one of the big dogs growls over the possession of a bone or some other treasure, Sasha quickly leaves and quietly seeks refuge under my legs). But when playing, Sasha maximizes her advantage of quickness and, paradoxically, her smaller size by advancing under the belly of the larger dogs and driving with her strong legs, hoists them off their feet.

Of course, Tioga uses *his* advantage of size by simply landing his full weight on Sasha's shoulders to subdue her. However, she quickly rolls over and bites his legs or even his belly, which customarily leads to his backing off. The three dogs take turns about which one will be "it" in their tooth-tag. Nootka usually volunteers to be the first victim, but a remarkable sense of justice leads the other two to take turns as the dog being bitten. The bites are remarkably benign, but the game is so persistent that the coat of each of them is quite wet after a few minutes.

Tioga is now much more aggressive than he was during his first year, but Sasha and Nootka seem to have a special relationship that at times excludes Tioga from the sisterhood.

By the time that first winter arrived, these three were closely bonded. When we went for a vacation, Sasha stayed with them in their large fenced-in yard in Marysville. When we returned to bring her home that first time, she made it clear that she liked it there just fine, and had to be placed on a leash in order to get her into our station wagon. (Of course, some of that is the chilly treatment which any owner encounters from a dog that has been "abandoned" by his heartless folks.) Although Sasha no longer prefers their house to ours, these three remain very fond of each other—a definite pack.

Although Ellie and I have skied for many years, our love of the downhill variety did not permit time to explore the cross-country, nordic type. But now, we had a compelling motive, to ski with Karl and Katie, and to exercise these three huskies, physically and socially. This required the acquisition of cross-country equipment, which meant a series of mistakes. The salesperson at REI, the mountaineering co-op, thought we wanted to ski on groomed, flat trails, and sold us the most narrow and light skis in stock, along with soft boots and bindings that might as well have been rubber bands. As expected, this equipment permitted skiing in a straight line, on smooth, flat terrain, but attempts at turning were humorous, as long as you were only watching.

The particularly tricky part was that there are not many flat areas in the Cascade Mountains, and when skiing down a logging road, acceleration is common. Approaching a sharp curve in a steep road was immensely entertaining for the audience. The choices were dictated by the speed of the skier: if the slope was quite mild, it was possible to step around the turn. Speed could not be controlled in the manner of downhill skiing by snow plow, since these skinny skis had no edges to speak of. Consequently, on a steeper road, Ellie would simply bail out before the turn by sitting down on the snow between the tails of the two skis. This works quite reasonably, except for the problem of regaining the upright position, which requires maneuvers quite distinct from those of downhill skiing, where the steepness of the hill allows you to literally roll down hill, back onto the skis.

The problems with cross-country conditions can be explained in terms of leverage. Your skis are not attached firmly to anything, and the poles appear to be made of aluminum foil—using them for leverage quickly produces gruesome angles. The temptation is to release the bindings so that you can use your feet in the fashion that God intended, but with the type we had been sold, that was much easier said than done, unlike the quick-release bindings we were accustomed to with downhill skiing.

Then there were the resuscitation efforts by three huskies, led by Nurse Nootka. It was plainly evident that a biped lying horizontally was mortally wounded, and mouth-to-mouth CPR was urgently required. It was also clear that this could best be administered if you firmly planted all four feet on the patient's chest and belly. Of course, there was a degree of competition in this CPR between the three doggies, which meant that sometimes one would be doing the mouth-to-mouth while the other two were alternately playing king-of-the-mountain on your chest.

In spite of all these difficulties, we soon became devoted to cross-country skiing. We couldn't go to the commercially groomed slopes, since they took extreme exception to the holes in the snow created by the 12 feet of our husky pack. That meant that the knowledge of logging roads that Ed and I had acquired in the course of a quarter of a century of climbing became useful. For example, Tonga Ridge parallels Highway 2 and begins where there is rarely snow, and continues up to the 4000 foot level at a benign grade that rarely is frightening on the down run, despite our flat-lander skis.

Even on logging roads, if we encountered other skiers, kvetching about the dogs was occasionally encountered. (Sometimes we environmentalists are insufferably intolerant!) We would point out to the complainers that they were free to go to the commercially groomed trails and we were not.

Ellie would have been more than content never to leave Beckler River Road, which meandered alongside the river for many miles, with scarcely any elevation gain, but its location at a low altitude meant that it was infrequently snow-covered, or was

A nordic outing in the springtime, above Lake Keechelus, in the background. (Photo by Ed Emery).

deeply rutted from 4-wheel drive vehicles. In short, we were "forced" to seek steeper and higher roads for our outings, which meant a return to the co-op for wider skis with metal edges, three point bindings, stiffer boots, and shorter and stronger poles.

The graduation of our outings to higher and steeper terrain did not bother Sasha in the least. She persisted in remaining in front, no matter how deep and unpacked the snow became, establishing her alpha-position in this motley pack.

The larger dogs were quite content with following, a most reasonable strategy since following the skiers allowed them to walk on partly packed snow (and sometimes the tails of skis). Even Tioga and Nootka would leave the packed snow for frequent forays into the woods, following Sasha, who was constantly alert to the possibilities of live critters or carrion left from a hunter's kill. There is little room for romantic ideas about huskies eating only fresh meat that they have personally killed; judging from Sasha, it seems that carrion is preferred, as I prefer an aged wine.

There are times in the winter, before the beginning and after the close of the commercial ski areas, when our pack can be taken to these areas. After closure of the lifts, the snow is still packed, and the wide, smooth runs permitted Karl to teach Ed and me how to make Telemark turns. For us expert downhill skiers, used to parallel turns and to serpentines in untracked powder, the Telemark turn was an abomination. But never underestimate the male's vulnerability to challenge! We have persisted, and I can now make lovely, linked Telemarks, at least on the packed snow of the ski areas.

Unfortunately, there are dangers to our dogs in the commercial ski areas. On a sunny April day when Sasha was two years old, our entire pack went to Stevens Pass. Dodging the snowmobiles was not a problem, although their fumes are unpleasant, but someone had left an unfinished sandwich near the treads of a snowcat that had not yet been put away for the summer. The machine had been well lubricated, and Sasha smeared against the grease, causing her white forelegs to turn a dirty bronze. She is not a dog that tolerates such ugly things on her person, and she attacked it with her tongue at every stop that day.

51

We only noticed a change in her behavior when we returned to our cars, when she promptly lay down away from the other dogs. This is unusual since Sasha rarely demonstrates fatigue after skiing outings, although her "nephew and niece" are likely to hop into Karl's Saab and sack out at the first opportunity.

By that evening and the following day, Sasha became alarmingly ill. She wouldn't eat, which alone suggested a serious disorder, and she was extremely agitated, unable to lie still for more than a few minutes. She panted, although it was quite cool in the house, and she looked desperate, since nothing she did made her feel better. There was no green grass to eat, her usual self-medication.

Of course, Doctor Campbell wasn't available, but his partner felt that, even if we weren't sure of the cause, that antibiotics were wise. Happily, she improved quickly, although I was convinced that it had nothing to do with the antibiotic. Nevertheless, the vet argued against stopping the treatment on the logical ground that it certainly wasn't hurting Sasha, and seemed to be helping. (As an academic pediatrician, there is always a concern about the overuse of antibiotics, but I have to agree with the vet's logic in this case, since it turned out well.)

Phil had said early in our discussions about this breed that they had an incredible resilience, and that he had begun to think of Ulu and Max as almost indestructible. I too had developed that comforting attitude, but I know they are not—they just act that way! Max was, in fact, killed by a speeding car when Sasha was only six months old.

At least I can report that Sasha has learned, and now if something foreign sticks to her fur, she does not try to lick it off, but lets it gradually wear off. For now, at least, I can pretend that my girl is immortal.

7

❖ SNIDELY THE CAT ❖

Snidely Whiplash was a boarder at our house long before Sasha. He was a Christmas gift from Renee to our eldest son Kurt, two years before they were married, but by the time Kurt moved out, Snidely had fully acclimated to our suburban life, with several acres of undeveloped hillside behind our house, complete with moles, voles, mice, squirrels, and birds.

He rarely spent much time in the house, preferring hunting, or simply lying in wait for whatever. He was never far away, judging from how quickly he materialized when one of us went out to get the paper, or on some other errand.

Kurt and Renee, in contrast, lived in "downtown" Mukilteo, with much more traffic, and they both worked. Consequently, when Kurt left our house there was a minor custody battle. Kurt loved his kitty, but that was our advantage—Snidely would have a better life at our place.

When the unruly puppy arrived, Snidely was almost seven years old. From the first, Snidely and Sasha had alternating days of dominance, much of that depending upon the specific terrain of encounter and their respective moods. Sasha was always taller, from the first day in our house, and when they were both on the floor the cat couldn't reach Sasha's face without leaping—a vulnerable posture when your opponent is equally quick. But if the cat was on a chair, or on a higher level on the stairs, he was formidable.

At our predinner snack time, Snidely learned to attend, although he was much less intense about food than Sasha. It was not uncommon for him to inspect a morsel of cheese tossed to him, and not eat it after thinking about it. He sometimes would conclude that the cheese was suitable bait for an ambush.

Sasha was invariably attracted to the cheese, which she regarded as hers since she was the one who conceived the tradition in the first place. Nevertheless, Sasha appeared to ask permission from Snidely, by circling in a non-belligerent stance, just out of reach of the cat's claws. As the circle tightened, sometimes Snidely would panic and bolt for the door.

At other times the feline would stay his ground until Sasha, driven to desperation, reached for the morsel, and then Snidely would unleash a lightning-quick swipe at her face. But Sasha rarely took a direct hit from Snidely's claws, or perhaps Snidely wisely decided that a truly angry Sasha would be dangerous and simply slapped with sheathed claws. (The record should show that he had never hesitated to use claws on his human hosts, suggesting either that he feared us less, or that we were less quick than Sasha.) I can remember only once seeing a tiny spot of blood on Sasha's muzzle after an exchange with Snidely.

In general, Sasha did not seem concerned about the cat's claws, particularly when she was trying to teach him to play, husky-style, when she would charge at the cat with a spectacular leap, landing on all fours, just outside the range of Snidely's claws. For this offense the cat would sometimes chase Sasha madly around the house, which is apparently what Sasha had in mind. Unfortunately for Sasha, the cat would not continue after one lap.

By the time Sasha was only five or six months old, she had decided that Snidely was, in some way she could not fathom, important to us, and that hurting the cat would be unacceptable behavior. That did not prevent her from reminding Snidely what *could* happen.

Sasha would casually walk by where the cat was sitting or standing and in an extraordinarily quick movement, envelop

Snidely's head completely, but harmlessly, in her mouth, then pull back with the pride of a fencer announcing "touché." Snidely could scarcely conceal his disgust.

That Sasha *could* do genuine violence to a creature of Snidely's size was demonstrated during her first year. On a summer's evening, well after dark, I took Sasha out for her bedtime potty. There was a faint rustling in the back of the lot, and Sasha unhesitatingly leapt into the bushes. There was no noise except for brief movement in the bushes, and Sasha emerged immediately with a very dead, but warm "ground beaver," a tailless creature of about ten pounds.

I was sorry to see a harmless animal die, but Sasha was enormously proud. She wasn't at all interested in eating it, but she was intent on keeping her trophy. It took a bribe with a generous piece of raw beef to get the poor creature's carcass away for a burial in a place Sasha could not reach.

I don't know whether Snidely witnessed the demise of the critter, but his relationship with Sasha continued to be secure. In fact, Snidely frequently brought home *his* catches and left the offering on the entrance deck where Sasha must pass on route to her morning "constitutional," and Sasha on more than one occasion would charge out to run off an alien aggressor cat challenging her Snidely.

Still, it would be an exaggeration to say that Sasha was fond of Snidely, but she certainly looked out for his interests in some ways, such as arranging for him to be let in during the period before we installed a pet door. Part of Sasha's motive may have related less to devotion to Snidely than to the fact that Snidely was frequently fed after being let in. His veterinarian special food is considered a delicacy by Sasha, who usually got her own half-dozen pellets when Snidely was fed.

This occasionally led to some rather involved maneuvers. Sasha would go to the front door to indicate that she wanted out; when the door was opened, there was Snidely, and Sasha clearly was not surprised. Occasionally, Snidely would demonstrate a fit of paranoia, with reluctance to enter the house, which would stimulate Sasha to go out and herd him into the house. As soon as

Snidely had entered the house, Sasha would run to the counter with Snidely's dish, and sit down at attention, waiting for *her* cat food.

There were times when no one was around and these two would lie close together in the sunshine, and on more than one occasion Snidely was detected brushing against Sasha's muzzle and purring. But Sasha is generally far more dedicated to play than affection, in contrast to Snidely who had an insatiable appetite for the latter.

At other times, Sasha became the enforcer for the cat's behavior. Whereas she is forbidden to be on the couch in our family room, Snidely assumed that the rules for the couch did not apply to him and would parade back and forth between Ellie and me, purring relentlessly, demanding to be stroked.

Sasha's light blue eyes would then become distinctly green, and she would jump up from her nearby position on the carpet and place her front legs on the edge of the couch (legal for her) and try to knock the cat over with one foot. The cat would usually retreat to the back of the couch, which Sasha sometimes accepted, but on other occasions, she would circle behind the couch to further harass the cat. Eventually, Snidely would retreat to his designated chair, and Sasha would lie back down with an apparent sense of accomplishment.

One major advantage Sasha enjoyed over her rival Snidely was that Snidely was totally incapable of catching popcorn in the air, a skill Sasha has honed to an art form. She almost never fails to catch a well-buttered morsel, something she can determine while it is still at its apogee.

If she is not hungry, she will simply not open her mouth when the unbuttered ones descend, allowing them to bounce off her muzzle. If she can't tell for certain whether it is adequately buttered, she will catch it, taste it, and if insufficiently buttered, expel the reject on the front of the couch.

Another advantage for Sasha is in the area of music appreciation. Unlike the comic strip pups that howl during classical music, Sasha seems oblivious to my hi-fi system, even when it is loud, which is more than I can say for Ellie. Of course, Sasha wasn't tested as thoroughly as Snidely.

Nap time for Sasha and Snidely, the cat. Note that the treacherous Snidely has surreptitiously taken control of Sasha's leash. (Photo by Ellie Guntheroth).

When our youngest son, Sten, was still home he had regular practices of his rock band at our house. Snidely was terrified by the band's music, and subsequently when rock music was played in his presence, live or recorded, he immediately ran toward the nearest exit and clawed frantically at the door, trying to escape.

Sten later graduated and entered the entrepreneurial world, and the musical milieu at our house settled down to mostly classical. Snidely would occasionally hear something on television that brought back the old panic, but Sasha pretends that she is completely deaf when it comes to music. Even Stravinsky's *Rites of Spring* doesn't cause her to stir.

Snidely, after 14 years of the good life, began to fade rather abruptly. His kidneys had failed, and he was taken for a last visit to Dr. Campbell. With Ellie holding him, he received an intravenous of soothing pentobarbital and simply relaxed; he went "gentle into the good night."

Although Ellie and I continue to see Snidely out of the corner of the eye, only to realize that it is a stuffed animal or something else, Sasha never searched for him, perhaps sensing his terminal condition. In fact, Sasha behaves as though Snidely had never existed, except that she still goes to his feeding station when she follows us downstairs to breakfast, and receives her pellets of Snidely's special diet.

8

❖ MORE CLIMBS ❖

Sasha's first night out.

In early September of the second year with Sasha, I decided to take her with me into the mountains for an overnight excursion. I selected two peaks that were on the same ridge, with the added advantages of having a trail that extended almost to the summit of the first one, and a small lake between the two for a camp site.

The weather was quite hot, and since the ridge is on the eastern slopes of the Cascades, completely dry. All of the streams that carry the snow melt in early summer had long since dried up, and there was no water on the trail up to the first peak. Sasha uses streams and lakes for cooling, as well as drinking, and it soon became obvious that she was travelling at a much slower pace than was her custom; she did not explore off trail, nor did she run much, but trotted methodically between shaded spots beneath the sparse pines and firs. She would flop down in the shade and pant, waiting for the old man to catch up. If I sat down to drink some Kool-Aid, she would sit close by and make clear that she wanted some water. It was the first time that I can recall that she had shown any interest in the contents of my pack other than for food.

Fortunately, I had brought extra water for her, but we still had to conserve, since she drinks almost the same amount of water as I, although she is one-third my weight. On this occasion I found that Kool-Aid with sucrose was quite acceptable to her, but later found that artificial sweeteners were not. (Perhaps she knows something that the Food and Drug Administration doesn't— only once has she become sufficiently thirsty to drink aspartame-sweetened water.)

After some hours, we reached the site of a former lookout, which was on the extreme eastern end of a ridge. The actual summit of Davis Peak was a quarter-mile west, and it was small and steep on all sides. It must have reminded Sasha of her very first summit, Mount Pilchuck, where I had picked her up and placed her on the walkway around the lookout. She was clearly anxious on this summit, with downfallen ears and tail, and she did not want to come close to me as I sat on the small summit. However, M&Ms overcame her paranoia about my intentions, and she finally inched her way onto the summit.

After my "obligatory" summit photos, we cautiously inched down, and she started back on the trail, the way we had come. When I started in the opposite direction, where there was no trail, she did not seem particularly reluctant to follow, and quickly regained the lead in the fashion of a true alpha-dog. This requires careful attention to my direction, with occasional adjustments of her vector, but rarely does she come all the way back to me unless I take a break.

We dropped through a gap just north of Davis, and then descended a rather tricky bit of down-sloping slab which was obviously worrisome to her. Nevertheless, when I continued, Sasha soon caught up and passed me again. In less than an hour we had descended to Opal Lake, and Sasha broke into a trot, leaving me well behind. She soon had waded into the water, took a long drink, and was swimming laps to cool off as I reached the shore.

This seldom-visited lake is not, in fact, opal colored but a dark blue with slight overtones of green. It nestles in a small cirque, with steep walls surrounding all but the eastern end, which opens onto a view of the Cle Elum valley. There was only a single fire ring, and no garbage of any sort, attesting to the difficulty in reaching the lake, and perhaps to the fact that the lake had few, if any, fish. Best of all, lush grass grew close to the lake between

Sasha on a rest break, in the shade, waiting for the old man to catch up.

boulders, promising a sheltered, soft bed for both of us.

I dropped my large pack, took out a small summit bag, and started around the northern wall of the cirque on the way to the next peak, Goat Mountain. It was only a couple of hours until we approached the gentle summit with Sasha in the lead once more. With no hesitation she trotted over to the very top, and sat down, facing the setting sun—and home. I wondered if she was just a little homesick

On our way back to Opal Lake she led all the way, following our scent, until we came to a slabby area that was obviously not to her liking. At that point, she came back to me and seemed to suggest that it was my turn now to lead. That was soon negotiated, but when we arrived back at the lake it was dark. In the tradition of the good cowboy who always feeds his horse first, I quickly got out Sasha's dog food—I failed to consider that horses aren't fond of cowboy food. In Sasha's case, feeding her first was a tactical error, since she regarded her serving as only an appetizer, and downed it quickly.

I tore open the plastic bags containing my freeze-dried dinner, and fired up the small, lightweight stove designed by Larry Penberthy. As I turned around, Sasha had her nose in my stroganoff, for which she received a rare slap, and a brief sermon. Shortly thereafter, she left to check out a nearby coney, a small, tailless critter that is a distant relative of the elephant.

After the stroganoff and a cup of coffee, I rolled out a pad and my sleeping bag on the grass. I had intentionally not brought a tent, but had simply forgotten to bring a bivvy sack; fortunately, the temperature was quite pleasant. I had brought a small square of blue foam for a pad for Sasha, in case we had to sleep on a bed of gravel or worse.

I patted the pad with my hand, telling her that this was for her, and she acknowledged that by doing the curious ritual circling for several turns, and then lying down in a tight curl with her nose tucked under her bushy tail. It appeared that we would have a restful night to restore our bodies, but about then, a full moon rose and Sasha rose, not to lie down again for the rest of the night.

It is difficult to explain how much I enjoyed that night. It was as beautiful a night and place as I can remember, and sharing it with my enthusiastic companion made it special. Sasha explored

On the summit of Goat Mountain, facing homeward, at dusk.

every inch of the cirque, trying to catch small things, but she never once barked or growled to spoil the silence. Once, however, I awoke to see her leaping gracefully over my head, at least five feet into the moon-drenched air. What she was pursuing never was apparent, although some interesting possibilities came to mind as I dozed off again.

She respected my sleep, as she does at home, and did nothing to wake me, but if I spoke to her, she would bestow a discrete kiss on the tip of my exposed nose. (She does not lap the whole of your face, but with exceptional precision touches only the very tip of your nose with the tip of her tongue. An exception is Karl's bearded face, which she laps extensively thinking, perhaps, that his muzzle is more like a proper dog's.)

With the warming sunrise, I sat up, and Sasha seemed particularly happy to see me. I don't quite understand the vocal and emotional greeting I always receive in those wonderful mornings in the mountains, but it is well worth the price of admission, since at home when I arise to go to work she is generally silent and aloof.

While I fired up the stove for a cup of hot coffee, Sasha made one final inventory of small beasties, and we soon started back up to the gap below Davis Peak. It was a glorious morning and Sasha was playful, showing no fatigue whatsoever. The steep slab was still formidable to her, and she complained anxiously when I climbed up it. I was unable to bribe her or invent any way to coax her up, but I finally hit on the idea of tying a light rope through her collar and leading her up through the rocks. It was as though she had a safe belay, and she cheerfully scrambled up and through the gap.

It was hot by the time we got back to the bridge leading to the Volvo wagon, and Sasha had a long wade in the river, and then crashed in the back of the wagon and slept all the way home. Dad, of course, had to drive. Sasha provided a new meaning to the old saw, "It's a dog's life."

Winter climbs.

That winter we were improving our cross-country skills, including the pack-of-three (Sasha, Tioga and Nootka). One of the items they had learned was that snow was useful as a water replacement; in fact, it was preferable to their palates. The only trick, soon learned, is not to eat too much at once, but to frequently scoop up a mouthful on the run—too much at one time leads to upchucking.

In the spring of that year Ed and I elected to try a snow climb of Silver Peak. As usual, Sasha maintained the lead up the three miles of trail. She can detect the location of a trail under several feet of snow, presumably by the human scent. (We must have a terribly strong one!) This skill is very useful in deep snow, when a switchback is indistinguishable from the terrain ahead.

Higher up, when we had left the trail, Sasha had to resort to porpoising as a means of locomotion in the deep drifts, since the snow had not compacted yet. When we got close to the ridge top, and the slope became quite steep, she retreated to just behind me. In a few places, even that position did not reassure her, and she would softly whine, inquiring if we didn't think that we were doing something foolish and macho. (She *is* female!)

Gaining confidence quickly, she was willing to explore on her own when we sat down for lunch on the summit of a ridge. We used this picture on our Christmas card that year. What is not evident from the print was that her canine tooth had made an imprint on this choice slide, the one she found literally to her taste.

Cannon Mountain.

In July of that year, Sasha and I again went on a climb without Ed. It was one of those peaks that look simple from the topographic map, with relatively gentle gradients, even though it was one of the taller peaks in the Enchantments at 8638 feet.

Beckey's guide book listed a route that would allow one to ascend a long ridge all the way to the top, a gain of over 5000 vertical feet.

Ed, Sasha and I had attempted this peak a month earlier, from the northwest side, and had been unable to find the summit in a blizzard. The peak was important for two reasons: we hadn't climbed it before, and the northwestern half of the mountain was outside the boundary of the Alpine Lakes Wilderness area, which meant it was legal for Sasha. This area was vigorously guarded by the Forest Service which has declared this to be off limits for dogs, and for more than a very limited number of humans at a time.

Consequently, when Sasha and I started out that morning we followed a logging road *away* from the parking lot that is the trailhead for Mountaineer Creek Trail; we planned to keep out of the restricted area, as good citizens. The first three thousand vertical feet were on the ridge, which was only partly wooded, but since it was on the north side of the mountain, heat was not a problem.

However, the higher we climbed, the more tortuous was the ridge. Consulting the altimeter and the contour map, it finally became clear that the ridge route was, in fact, a fantasy. We were facing near-vertical walls that blocked the ridge, and the only route that was non-technical required a descent of 600 feet into the Wilderness Area, skirting the west side of still-frozen Coney Lake. The summit looked attainable, but the challenge was obvious: a long and steep couloir led back up a thousand feet from the lake to the plateau just below the summit.

On the snow in the basin, around the lake, and up the first few hundred feet, Sasha was well in front. Only the top inch or two of the snow was soft and she had to use her claws at times to keep from sliding on the hard snow, an increasing problem as we climbed higher and the couloir became progressively steeper.

By the time we had climbed two-thirds of the way up, Sasha began having serious doubts about the entire plan. I must admit that I too was becoming concerned about the pitch, and in particular began to think about how unpleasant its descent would be. Sasha began to lead toward a ledge with easy access from the snow in the couloir, unlike most of the rock next to the snow which was either vertical or guarded by a moat, or both. She exited the snow and sat down on a relatively flat rock and whined softly. It occurred to me that if the rangers wanted to expel us from the area we wouldn't really object, subject to acceptable transportation.

After a brief rest, a shared candy bar, and careful weighing of the alternatives, I concluded that the only realistic solution was to continue up the snow with the hope that we could find an easier way down from the plateau than this couloir. Sasha watched attentively as I carefully stepped back onto the steep snow, kicking each step with my Galibier boots, and advancing slowly with two hands on my ice axe. Sasha immediately accepted my lead, and followed closely, nose almost touching my calf; she did not stray one inch out of my steps until we climbed past the lip of the couloir, when she instantly reclaimed the lead, as though she had never harbored doubts or fears.

We had emerged on Druid Plateau, a spacious scene, free of snow in spite of the altitude of 8500 feet. The horizon was composed of the ragged granite peaks and ridges of the Stuart range and Cashmere Crags, an area called the Enchantment Lakes, offering some of the best climbing in the state. Under foot, on first glance, there appeared to be no sign of life. The grayish, coarse sand was vermiculite derived from the abundant granite—a moonscape came to mind. Looking closer, there were tiny forms of many wild flowers, including charming little lupine.

Only a hundred feet away was the summit block. After a couple of hundred feet of vertical gain over some lichen-crusted granite blocks, I was standing on the small summit. Sasha would have nothing to do with this one, and the more I would entreat her to share my tiny platform, the farther away she would edge, evidence of persisting Pilchuck paranoia.

By this time, it was 3 o'clock, and we had been climbing for seven hours; I began to think about the time it would take to get back to the car. Clearly, if it took us as long to get down as to climb up, we were going to run out of daylight, and speed going down the couloir was not desirable. Based on several experiences indelibly etched into my mind by high levels of circulating adrenaline, I knew that it was generally better to return by the ascent route, since that had the advantage of familiarity. Against that consideration was the steepness of this thousand foot couloir, ending in the lake. I deduced that Sasha would be quite reluctant to start down that snow, although if I were alone I would have chosen that route, since I had an ice axe for self-arrest.

In short, it was time to look carefully at the contour map for another descent route. Incredibly enough, about a half-mile to the east, the xeroxed map from Beckey's guide showed a dotted line between two ridges that appeared to be a trail—it wasn't,

On a wintry ridge.

only a "climber's route"—and the gradient on the topog foretold
no problems.

At this point, a sane person, knowing that Charlie Brown *never*
will get to kick the football with Lucy holding it, would guess that
there was only a small chance that the route even existed, and an
even smaller possibility that it would be easy. Worst of all, once
committed to the route at this hour, there was no chance that
backtracking would get us out that night. But like Charlie Brown, I
decided that just this once, Lucy would not pull the ball away at
the last minute, and Sasha and I would make it back to the car in
daylight to spare.

The first half mile on the plateau was pleasant enough, and

the first long gully down was no real problem, although it was very dry and dusty, with loose rock—one of Sasha's least favorite environments. But after that, there was a second, lovely plateau. I thought I had discovered a virtual Garden of Eden. There were numerous alpine fir and hemlock, with their dark green, set off by the brighter green of lush, tall grass everywhere, interspersed with lupine and daisies. (At this altitude, it was spring. One of the joys of climbing is that, if you climb high enough, it will be spring, or even winter, no matter the month!)

There were deciduous larches, whose spectacular yellow needles later in September create unbelievably beautiful backgrounds for the many turquoise lakes here in the Enchantments, but in July the larch blend modestly into all the other evergreens. Crystal clear brooks crisscrossed the meadow, a welcome foot-cooler for Sasha and only a vigorous step-across for me. I hadn't thought much about the altitude—it was 6000 feet—but thought only of the isolation and beauty of this meadow, and how I wanted to bring Ellie up there to share this special place. It had not occurred to me that there would be substantial difficulties in getting there from the trail, since the contour map showed a gradual gradient all the way to Mountaineer Creek.

There may have been a better route than the one we took down from this paradise, but ours was between two large streams, and the "gradual" descent was actually an unending succession of cliffs. Incredibly, in each of the infinite number of cliffs there was an oblique ramp down one side or the other.

Since Sasha was much faster, she sped up the process substantially by checking out the alternatives; if she came back from the left side of a cliff, I could count on that being impassible, and I would proceed to the right side. (Rapelling was out of the question on two accounts: Sasha would have been unwilling, and I had no rope with me.)

Of course, each of these ramps was thoroughly congested with scrub cedar, salmonberry bushes with their thorns, ferns which obscured the footing, and vine maple, and when the ramp was too close to one or the other of the streams, devil's club.

Devil's club is a plant that prefers rocky, wet places near

stream beds or swamps, places as unfavorable for the climber as they are favorable for this weed. When struggling over slippery rocks, the tendency is to grasp for anything that will prevent sliding over a cliff or into the stream. Unless the climber is a slow learner, he or she will grab blindly in that situation only once! For the next two or three weeks, the tiny thorns from the devil's club will cause pain any time something is grasped firmly, as the barbs bury themselves ever deeper into the palms and finger pads.

After my first encounter some 30 years ago, this plant has assumed a malicious character in my mind, and not altogether facetiously, I think that I would fall to my death before I would again grasp a devil's club.

Meanwhile, Sasha and I continued slowly down some 3000 feet of this harsh terrain as the sun rapidly descended. Sasha was patient, and never seemed anxious, although I continually estimated and re-estimated how dark it would be when we hit the trail by the river. From the map, I thought that we would intersect the river fairly close to the point at which the trail crossed to the other side. Unfortunately, the river valley was fairly broad when we reached it, and swampy in places.

Worst of all, when we reached the river, the trail was on the *other* side, and the stream was too deep and fast to ford. Although the bridge was no more than a quarter-mile down stream, getting to it and the trail required at least a half-hour struggle in failing light. The dense brush was easily the worst part of the whole trip, and at times seemed diabolically motivated, as though we were being punished.

The sun had gone behind the mountain ridges by the time we reached the river bank, and by the time we reached the trail, it was dark. Fortunately it was a good trail, although forbidden to doggies, and I rehearsed my lines in case I ran into a ranger. I planned to tell him how we had gone to great lengths to avoid violating the boundaries, even to the extent of risking our lives, and that we had descended to the trail as a last resort. My anger as I thought of this great injustice helped propel my weary bones the last two miles back to the car. I was almost sorry that I didn't run into a ranger to tell him or her of my low esteem of their operation of the Enchantments.

The drive back into Leavenworth was uneventful, and I found a deli that was about to close. They had a surplus of fried chicken for which they charged only half the regular price, which meant that Sasha ate very well. I did have some worries about her eating the bones; it isn't that I really think chicken bones are dangerous for a pup that chews everything well, but I knew only too well the guilt I would experience if I was responsible for any evil chicken bones. (I have frequently argued that in the wild, coyotes and wolves regularly eat birds if they are lucky enough to catch them but Ellie responds that cooking the birds creates a brittle, more dangerous bone.)

It was well after midnight when the sleeping pup and the

A typical view of Sasha near any summit, looking down on her slower companion.

sleepy dad rolled into the garage, heroic survivors of a self-imposed ordeal on Cannon Mountain. We had no regrets, but I never proposed that Ellie should go with us to see our Garden of Eden.

Rudderham Mountain. The cliff.

Just as the experiences of climbing create strong bonds between climbers that have shared them, the bond between Sasha and me became stronger with each peak shared, and I increasingly thought of ways to include her in my plans. That summer of Cannon Mountain, I left her home only a couple of times while I climbed. Two of these were technical climbs with rope and chockstones, including the thoroughly unpleasant north face of Mount Index, the longest vertical "bushwhack" known to me.

North Gardner would have been a perfect climb for Sasha, but that trip was scheduled during her recuperation from the snowcat grease. With that peak, and Dragontail in August of that year, I had climbed all of the highest 25 peaks in the state, and I began to look more favorably on peaks that were non-technical climbs. Rudderham seemed such a peak.

The approach was by the Money Creek Road, a long and scenic logging road ending at Lake Elizabeth, a favorite for local fishermen, but not for city people because of the length and roughness of the road. Rudderham was almost entirely forested on the southern slope that we planned to ascend, and the trees were mostly old growth, whose continual shade killed off most of the brush, making for relatively easy travel.

We had been moving quite rapidly up hill for about three hours when we encountered a hundred-foot cliff. It wasn't a particularly sheer face, which is why the contour map failed to show it, but there were vertical steps of 20 to 30 feet that required modest skill in rock climbing, and definitely required hands with opposable thumbs, one of the few talents that Sasha lacks.

The two of us explored for at least a hundred yards in either direction seeking a way around the cliff but found none. Thinking I was fairly close to the summit, I decided to leave her on "stay" while I climbed the face. She did not complain, but she continued to explore laterally for a way up.

I was not as close to the summit as I had thought, and the minutes raced by as I continued my ascent without Sasha. Forty-five minutes had elapsed before I reached the summit, and I was definitely anxious about her, hoping that she wouldn't stray off and get lost. (As I now know, she is much less likely than I to get lost, but I felt guilty in any case.)

I quickly took the obligatory summit shots with my Minolta, and was putting the pack back on when I heard one of my favorite sounds, Sasha panting. She was unusually tired and hot, but still going at a trot. I don't know how far laterally she had been forced to go to get around the cliff, but it was a remarkable feat to find me on this featureless long ridge, with a summit area that stood out by only a few extra vertical feet. I presume it was by scent, and a gift of great precision about her own location.

Whether this sense of where she is relates to the car, or to some more general reference system would be interesting to know. An additional skill that she clearly demonstrates regularly is memorizing where she has been, and how to return there. All of these skills—and her intelligence—make her a highly competent navigator.

We had a happy reunion, and descended to the nearest shade, which happily also included a patch of snow, where she plopped down on her belly and bit off chunks of snow. She was sufficiently hot and winded that it was several minutes before she showed interest in my lunch.

On our descent, we had to go more than a quarter-mile laterally to find a way around the cliffs. She was content to follow on the way down, so I am uncertain where she ascended the cliff.

A solo ascent of Mount Si.

The following winter a German medical student, Rüdiger Lohmann, came to work with me to study and to do research on crib death. I have rarely met a more organized and enthusiastic student, and to make things even better, he was eager to learn cross-country skiing and climbing. Since he was already accomplished as a downhill skier, the cross-country skills were quickly acquired. He also was fond of dogs and quickly became good friends with Sasha.

Early that spring Ed and I took Rüdiger up the four mile trail to Mount Si for a taste of snow climbing. Instead of climbing up the steep northeast-side gully, the standard route, we dropped into the shallow but broad bowl on the south side. It was no problem for Rüdiger, and he quickly mastered the use of an ice axe. Sasha thought it was a piece of cake, and long preceded us to the ridge, where she found a strategic rock for lounging while she watched us labor up the snow.

When we caught up, another reason for her waiting was apparent, a difficult step-across that was mildly exposed—a climber's way of saying that if you slip, you will be very sorry, but only briefly! Sasha tried various ways around this obstruction, but found them all unacceptable, so she simply waited to see what we would do. It wasn't too bad for us since there were reasonable handholds, but then we had to persuade her.

Nothing convinced her until I got out the short leash and attached it to her collar. Once again, she responded as though she had a secure belay, and immediately jumped across. It was reassuring to see that Sasha had her own standards of safety. (This past summer, an unfortunate dog wearing a backpack attempted this step-across, but a protruding side pocket struck the cliff wall, causing him to fall to his death.)

Later in the spring, when the snow was off Mount Si, we returned to give Rüdiger his first experience with roped climbing. We started up the east face of the "haystack," a 200 foot wall, and I led up a 75 foot crack on its southern end. After I found a good belay spot, I brought up Rüdiger, while Ed stayed below with Sasha. After a half-hour, we arrived at the rocky summit, to be greeted by Sasha. I thought that Ed must have brought her up the standard route on the north side, but Ed was nowhere in sight. (He had chosen to come up behind Rüdiger, unroped.)

Sasha had not waited for us, and decided that the route she had learned some months before probably led to the same place we were heading. Accordingly, she had descended into the southern bowl, and had preceded all of us to the summit. She wasn't even panting, and had already investigated the lunches of two or three climbers on the summit.

By now, Sasha's skills in climbing, coupled with her alpha-personality, permitted her to be the first on the summit regularly, sometimes by as much as 15 minutes, from where she looked down with pride.

The worst climb: Osceola.

We had never climbed in the northeast corner of the Cascades in north central Washington because of its remoteness and Ed and I made ambitious plans to climb several of the relatively high peaks there in July of 1989. We made our first attempt on July first, but when we reached Hart's Pass, there was still too much snow on the road to permit driving all the way to our starting place, Slate Pass. It was raining and snowing, with poor visibility, and we reluctantly settled for a soggy hike to Slate Peak and Haystack Peak, simple walk-ups.

We returned almost a month later, and were surprised to find there was almost no snow in sight, even on our objectives, which were over 8500 feet in elevation. At least it wasn't raining! We put Sasha's new backpack on, and she assumed an air of total martyrdom, with drooping ears and tail, although the weight was relatively less for her weight than our packs were for our weight.

She did far less exploring while wearing her burdensome pack, but when we reached the valley bottom and Robinson Creek, she waded in and gave a new meaning to the pack's waterproof label: the fabric *held* water quite well, after it filled! Of course, we took off the pack, emptied it of the free water, and put it back on. Fortunately, her dried food was wrapped reasonably well, and stayed almost dry. Unfortunately, water is not the only hazard of these packs. Sasha spends much of her time off the trail, and has an excellent sense of what she can squeeze beneath or under. The pack extended a few inches beyond her usual boundaries, which she did not allow for, and at frequent intervals she would emerge from the bushes with the pack hanging off to one side, or upside down.

I soon realized that I was spending more energy to keep the pack on in its proper position than the energy required to carry her food and water in my backpack, although on this trip I remained firm.

It was a long ten miles for all of us before we camped. As soon as we relieved her of her pack, she began stalking chipmunks, and she did not sleep at all that night. The next day, all of us donned our packs and we climbed up to lovely Lake Doris, at 7100 feet. We found a camp site, unloaded our packs, and started up our first objective, Osceola.

We had caught glimpses of this mountain as we hiked in, and we knew that there was not a snowball's worth of snow on it, but now we perceived the worst: this huge massif was composed of an infinite number of rocks, few of them more than a foot in diameter. Not only was this a vertical junkyard, the rocks were incredibly unstable.

I cannot remember a more tedious climb, but my boredom was nothing compared to what was happening to Sasha's paws. On the way down, she would frequently stop and whine softly. I would extend my apologies, but the fact was that there were no reasonable alternatives to continuing down, and when we returned to Lake Doris, she spent a *long* time wading and cooling her feet.

It was mid afternoon when we got the tent up; it was hot in spite of the altitude. The ecology of the lake at this time was per-

Sasha with her dreaded red pack.

fect for insects, and both mosquitoes and deer flies were swarming. Ed and I put on repellent, but Sasha would have nothing to do with such smelly stuff. (She has since learned that repellant does help, and submits to applications to her ears and forehead, and below her eyes.)

On this hot, July day, Sasha was more miserable than I have ever seen her. She did not seem to feel the mosquito bites, and soon her face was distorted, her eyes almost swollen shut. The flies plagued her more, and she constantly tried to bite them in mid-air, with variable luck.

She wanted desperately to nap after two days of climbing and a night with little or no sleep. Her eyes would almost close, and her head would start dropping toward the ground, when a fly would land on her nose.

If you have never known the torture of these flies, count yourself fortunate. These Kamikaze-like insects are relentless and reckless, with a willingness to die for their meal, and no repellent seems to faze them. It is easy to understand horses and cows panicking and stampeding after a few hours of their torture. Sasha usually encountered deer flies on the trail where she was not a "captive audience" but in camp in the heat of day she was at their mercy—a trait notably lacking in deer flies.

Just watching her became torture and I tried various strategies to protect her, such as bringing her into our tent. The tent was too hot, and in any case, Sasha was more than a little paranoid about it and would not stay inside. By sundown we had decided, with no dissenting opinion, not to go after the other two piles of rubble that were on our itinerary—we wanted only to escape.

Somehow, we all made it through the night, and by the next day, when we started back, Sasha seemed no worse for wear. So much for the mountains of north central Washington.

Dog-eating horses and other mountain creatures.
Several of our climbs took us to the other side of the Cascades, in part to escape the seemingly endless rain in western Washington. This is also the territory of fierce animals, particularly the giant carnivore, the horse!

Sasha and a dog-eating horse.

Sasha's first encounter was when she was only a year old and it was the first time I had heard her bark when we were on a trail. (Her encounters with porcupines were on logging roads or in campsites.) She was fascinated by these fearful creatures who were so much larger than dogs or men, and unlike the rare deer she encountered, they did not run away.

One day, after we had climbed Jolly Mountain, the trail back led by a corral with three horses behind a rail fence. This time she did not bark, but sat watching near Ed and me as we changed from our boots and drank our cold drinks from the cooler. One horse was obviously familiar with dogs, and stood at the railing and did not move away as Sasha gradually crept closer. Finally she was just across the railings from his deadly hooves, more "wired" than I have ever seen her, moving an inch or so forward, but ready for retreat at the slightest hint of aggression.

This was a sly old horse, with what would pass for a sense of humor. He slowly lowered his head and gave a sudden, long and shrill whinny. Sasha literally jumped five feet in the air, and was out of there!

Now that she is older and more sophisticated, she no longer barks at these animals, but she still is *very* interested in them. I harbor concerns about her with horses because she seems completely unaware of the danger of approaching horses from behind, an approach favored by her based on an erroneous idea that they don't know she is even there.

Some of the other animals that Sasha finds interesting are unknown to me, but they have burrows that provide Sasha with endless entertainment and exercise. I have watched her sit patiently for a half-hour close to a rocky entrance to the burrow of a chipmunk, and she would have stayed longer, but I was leaving. If the burrow is in soft ground, Sasha is an indefatigable digger. If she encounters a root, she bites it off. After a stint at digging in the usual posture, with alternating scoops of her powerful front legs, she will lie on her side and continue with the excavation. If the earth is really soft, she will dig for hours, long after we have entered our tent for the night.

Needless to say, Sasha likes to stay outside the tent, even if it is raining, since outside is where the action is. On one occasion, she burrowed under our tent, which amused me but not old Ed, who claims to be a light sleeper.

Squirrels are of special interest to Sasha if they are on the ground. She has accepted the heavy responsibility of enforcing Sasha's Law: no squirrel shall remain on the ground in her presence. As soon as they have scrambled up the closest tree, she promptly trots back to the trail with every appearance of satisfaction in a job well done. The squirrels invariably have a few harsh comments about her ancestry, but their opinion is not esteemed by Sasha.

On the other hand, when she is in her own yard, she will sit quietly for hours watching the squirrels in the trees. She has never forgotten that one fell out of a tree when two squirrels were fighting. Sasha almost caught that one, and she has been hoping for another chance ever since.

Chasing squirrels in the city may be hazardous to your health. Once, when Sasha accompanied me to the climbing rock on the University campus, I tied her to a post with a stretch cord (a twangy-boinger, in the words of my sons), and a reel with a cord of some 30 feet. While I practiced varying climbing routes on the rock, she sat quietly watching a squirrel in a tree that was 50 feet away. The squirrel—nobody ever claimed that squirrels were intelligent—decided that he would move to the next tree, on the ground. His path placed him within 40 feet of Sasha, and she forgot entirely about the cord.

She accelerated remarkably, and by the time she had reached the end of the reel, she had reached a handsome velocity. I looked up just as she hit the end of the cord. Her leather collar might have broken a less sturdy neck, but Sasha looked wonderfully surprised as she did a complete flip, landing on her feet, with her tail closest to the squirrel, who was running back toward the tree with conviction. To this day, when Sasha is at the rock, she sits quietly, and *never* runs after squirrels in that venue.

Some hikers and climbers argue against allowing dogs in the Wilderness on the grounds that dogs disturb the wild animals. Of course Sasha disturbs the squirrels, and on rare occasion has startled a deer into flight. In the latter case, she returns after a brief chase, sensing the futility of a single canine—even a *lupus*—keeping up with these fleet animals.

It strikes me that the last thing a true conservationist should want to do is to tame these wild creatures, big and small. The incredible fact is that official Wilderness Areas are open to hunting! (When I wrote to confirm that and to point out the contradiction between permitting hunting but not dogs, the ranger replied that they could never have gotten the Wilderness legislation passed if they hadn't exempted hunting.) It seems to me that Sasha does the wild animals a genuine service to remind them that dog's best friend, man, is apt to be the deadliest of all animals.

9

❖ THE REUNIONS ❖

It was surprisingly difficult to achieve bonding with Sasha when we first adopted her at three months of age. From her perspective, we had pupnapped her, and we were a poor substitute for her mother Ulu and her brother Woot. To make matters worse for us, she had bonded firmly with Phil and Jeanne, in spite of her tender age.

During the early weeks and months with us, Phil would drop by to check on her progress and to reintroduce her to her mother and brother. It was then we could observe the extent of her devotion to Phil. In a submissive manner—typical for huskies, but which we never had seen before—Sasha would drop to the ground, squirm on her belly, and crawl toward him, urinating. This painful sight reminded Ellie and me of how little she really thought of us, and how she hoped at last to be reunited with her *real* family.

We finally asked Phil not to visit Sasha for a while, hoping that she would more quickly bond with her doting step-parents. (Lorenz warns of this failure to re-bond in the older husky, but seems to have underestimated the problem in puppies.)

Some months went by before the next visit with her real family, and this time it seemed more like a meeting with old friends, without the belly crawl. After Phil and Jeanne had their baby, we felt secure enough to propose an all-purpose reunion with Phil, Jeanne, and their two Siberian huskies and Karl, Katie, and their two malamutes, and of course, Sasha! It was a great social success for the Princess, who knew *everyone*, whereas the two canine couples knew only her. Ulu was by now 10 years old, and stood off from the rest, enjoying the party more or less vicariously.

While we packed snow for parking places for the three vehicles at the start of the Eagle Creek Road, the dogs began the process of sorting out the dominance thing. Woot has a much thicker coat than does his sister Sasha, and looks much heavier than she—in fact, he weighs at least 20 pounds more than she, and had long before demonstrated his dominance over her, something of no great importance to Sasha.

Similarly, Tioga was big enough that he was unconcerned about *anyone*, and was his usual laid-back self. Nootka, who never met a dog she liked except for Sasha and her brother Tioga, had selected Woot as her personal challenge, and was stalking around him, stiff-legged with her ruff up.

The first combat occurred before we had even left the cars, and Woot won quickly. They were then separated by Karl by simply hooking up his two dogs to himself for *skijoring*, which occupied Nootka adequately. Ellie hooked up Sasha for a trial of *skijoring*, which was fascinating to watch. Whereas Sasha had been wandering all over the road and frequently off the road, she now pulled straight in the center of the road, as though she had always pulled a sled or a skier. However, she would stop immediately if Ellie quit poling—if Ellie poled, Sasha would take off at a steady pace more rapid than Ellie was comfortable with, so Sasha regained her freedom in short order.

By noon, there had been two more skirmishes between Woot and Nootka with Woot winning each of them, but it was evident that Nootka was smouldering and had by no means accepted his dominance; after all, at stake was the admiration and love of her Sasha, who looked on their confrontations with only a hint of interest. At noon, the party stopped for lunch. The five dogs were milling around close to each other when Nootka launched her last—and best—attack.

Much to everyone's surprise, particularly Woot's, Woot finished on the bottom, and quickly indicated submission. It may have been fortunate that Phil and Jeanne decided to head back at that time, since they still had a long trip to their home on Bainbridge Island, or there may have been demands for a rematch. Although Woot may be less dedicated to the top dog position than Nootka, there is no doubt in my mind that Nootka would never permanently accept a subordinate position.

With the anthropomorphism peculiar to pet owners, I concluded that Sasha was pleased that her "niece" had bested her pushy brother. (I should add that there was no broken skin or any hint of physical injury to either Woot or Nootka; there is no need to injure to sort out the hierarchy of a pack of huskies.)

Lunch with just Nootka, Tioga, and Sasha was as peaceful as it always is. Sasha is a shameless and effective moocher, with a highly developed sense about who has what goodie, and how much is left, and when to move to another. She knows that I do not share with her until the last bite, a strategy to limit her intense lobbying, but as she sees the size of the sandwich diminishing, her pressure increases proportionately.

Nootka and Tioga, on the other hand, are trained not to beg by Katie and Karl, but it is a real test of their character to watch Sasha working the field, and succeeding. The actual effect of all this is that Nootka and Tioga actually have learned to beg by sitting a few feet away, and looking wonderfully sad; it seems quite effective, at least when applied to pushovers.

After our lunch on the road overlooking sunny Eagle Creek valley, we elected to ski on up the road. We soon reached an avalanche track which had swept across the road and filled it. That became our turn around spot, and Ed, Katie, and Ellie started back down, while Karl and I tried a few Telemark turns off the side of the road where the slope was not too steep and the trees were not too thick. The downhill part was brief, frequently ending in a crash and it was a slow process climbing back up to the road.

At some point we became aware that we were not getting the usual canine resuscitation when we were down in the snow, but we dismissed our doubts on the grounds that the dogs were with

Ed. Sasha can be counted on to be at the front of any activity, and her "niece and nephew" usually follow in deference to her greater experience as a mountain dog.

After a half-hour of Telemarks, Karl and I began skiing back down the logging road, trying to catch up. After a couple of miles we could see the three skiers below us as the road switched back and forth, but we couldn't make out the dogs. After some shouting we determined that the pups were not with them and worse, they hadn't seen them since lunchtime. They assumed the dogs were with us!

Karl and I left our packs at the side of the road and began the push up the hill again, noting with concern the lengthening shadows. We tried to recall exactly when we had seen them last, and agreed that it was before we turned around, and that Sasha was seen heading off the road, uphill, and that the two younger dogs had probably followed.

Sasha has always had an extraordinary nose for carrion, which provokes a very positive response in her, akin to the effect on me of cooking garlic. When she locates the carrion, she knows that we won't approve, and she gorges as quickly as possible.

About 45 minutes up the road Karl and I met the trio struggling down the road toward us, with Sasha in the lead, badly hobbled by her sled harness which had come off partially, so that she tripped on it every step of the way. She was, however, moving consistently, if slowly. Tioga was *very* tired, and would stop regularly to rest and Nootka was trying to stay with both of them. Surprisingly, Sasha did not look especially stressed by the fact that she was hobbled, but appeared to be embarrassed, as she usually does when she has made a rare mistake in navigation.

She wasn't at all reluctant to have me take off her harness and carry it. We shortly ran into another couple who reported that they had met the dogs at the very end of our trail, by the avalanche. Apparently, when the dogs returned to the road from their carrion they followed our scent *up* the road—Sasha was already tangled in her harness at that point. She declined their offer to untangle her and had struggled on. Although she couldn't tell initially whether our tracks were going up or down hill, she could tell when she got

to the end of our uphill tracks. If we had waited at the bottom she
would have safely delivered her two charges to us, but I was
pleased with our efforts to find them and to be able to help Sasha
untangle. In spite of her extremely inefficient locomotion, she was
less tired than Nootka or Tioga, and she assumed the lead the rest
of the way.

Of course, it was downhill, and since I was on skis, I began to
gain on her. As usual, she was running in the tracks, where the
footing was more solid. On most days, as I overtake her I begin to
make a sound like a siren, which stimulates her to go even faster.

She tried speeding up on this day, but for the first time just
couldn't quite do it, and she suddenly dropped to the snow in as
low a profile as possible, with her ears tucked back. Considering
my poor control on Nordic skis at the time, she and I were fortunate that I was able to ski over and around her by separating my
skis a little more. After that, I stopped more often to wait for her.

Karl had to stop even more frequently for Tioga, but we all
got back to the cars with plenty of daylight. Even Sasha jumped
into the car as soon as we opened the back, and all the pups had
an unusually quiet ride home. All's well that ends well!

Sledding.

Sasha's second reunion with Woot and Ulu was just two
years later. Phil had built a small cabin north of Lake Wenatchee,
across Stevens Pass to the dryer snow east of the Cascade crest.
His home on Bainbridge Island almost never got snow, and you
can't practice a dog-sled team if you haven't got snow. With the
cabin Phil had acquired a miniature dog sled, revealing his plan.

The sled was just the right size for a child, such as his Johnny,
who was three years old. Phil had been eager to try teaming Sasha
with Woot the year earlier, but that had been a very poor year for
snow in the northwest.

This Sunday I drove Ed, Ellie and Sasha over from a cloudy
Seattle, and we left the clouds at Stevens Pass. We drove past the
lake in brilliant sunshine reflected off of a couple of feet of new
snow. This was a day *made* for sledding and skiing.

Ulu, as befitted her advanced years, was excused from being

Sasha, on the right, and her brother Woot pulling 3-year-old Johnny.

hitched up, but Sasha and Woot were more than willing. They were excited—very excited! I had been taught in psychology courses that "instincts" were not characteristic of higher animals, and that dogs' behavior was almost entirely learned. But watching Sasha who had never before seen a sled, not to mention being hooked up to one, contradicted my instructor's beliefs. Whereas Sasha's normal course in proceeding down a road or trail is a random wandering from side to side, she and Woot proceeded straight-as-an-arrow down this wide, snow-covered road.

They were running at such a rate that I quickly became winded, and had to stand on the brakes at the end of the sled. Woot immediately began to howl, and Sasha continued to try to move the sled, brakes and all.

Meanwhile, Ulu brought tears to our eyes as she jumped over the traces and stood immediately behind the two young dogs, showing her willingness, arthritis and all, to do her part to pull the

sled. I thought of the sadness of "Old Dog Tray" when he was retired from pulling his cart.

Evidence that relatively advanced animals such as dogs are
"hard wired" for certain behavior can also be found in sheep-herd-
ing dogs. A close friend and colleague in the Physiology Depart-
ment acquired a young Keltie who had never seen a sheep. Al sus-
pected innate behavior from the first time he allowed the pup to
accompany him as he rode his bike. The dog nearly killed both of
them with his frantic attempts to herd the erratic bicycle.

Not long after that, he took him to a convention of this breed
in sheep country, and when the dog was let loose with a small
band of sheep, immediately began to round them up into a tight
herd.

I cannot explain how activity such as pulling a sled or herding
sheep can be encoded onto genes, but I have no doubt that it occurs. I also have no doubt that working dogs really like their work,
and that dog-sled racing can be regarded as cruelty to animals only
by someone who has not seen the joy in the dogs' faces as they
head out, with smiles and laid-back ears.

Most of the time, the closest Sasha comes to work is climbing
with me. I am aware that my reasons for climbing are complicated
and to some extent intellectual: to exercise my body to keep it
alive and working well and to accumulate "honors" by piling up
peaks bagged. But there is something deep down that is compelling. Like any desire, even the most primitive, there are times
when I am satiated, and can comfortably go a couple of weeks
without thinking about the mountains, particularly if the weather is
bad. But then, I feel a persistent hunger that won't be appeased
until I am in the mountains again.

I think that Sasha also has a similar cycle: when she comes
home from a long or tedious climb, it is clear that if I wanted to go
again too soon, that she would be not eager, perhaps reluctant.
But if she misses a week or two, she shows a genuine anxiety
about whether she can come when I start preparing for an outing.
In short, she expresses her wanderlust as a desire for the mountains in contrast to Thomas' Mischa, who had nothing more exciting than the streets of Cambridge.

Departure.

In the months after our reunion near Lake Wenatchee, Ulu began to fade. At 15, it was more than just arthritis. She was losing her hearing, and her memory was not so good, and the most humiliating to her, her bladder control was unpredictable. But she continued to love her outings with her family, and was visibly distressed to be left behind. Phil thoughtfully picked trail hikes with no cross-country travel, and set a modest pace.

Early in that fall they were all on Nason Ridge hiking in crisp, sunny fall weather, when Phil and Jeanne noticed that Ulu wasn't with them. This is not unusual for huskies—hiking with people doesn't mean continuous contact with them—the dog is usually ahead, at the limit of visual contact. The controlling factor is the dog's vision, not the human's, and there will be periods of several minutes when the human part of the team doesn't see his canine companion.

Consequently, exactly where Ulu was when last seen is not clear, but her disappearance was quiet, with dignity, and final. She apparently had decided that it was time to leave her family and just laid down somewhere off the trail, in mountains so familiar to her.

Phil and Jeanne searched immediately, and they continued to search for the next three days. Although they were aware of the way of huskies who go off to die alone, they feared that she might have only been lost, alive but confused, and hungry or thirsty— they simply had to search.

Whether these dogs wish to spare their family from these final minutes, or are simply seeking quiet and solitude is unknown, but I am certain that Ulu would not have predicted or wanted her family to be upset by her departure. Woot must have understood where Ulu had gone. He did not join in the search, either that afternoon or the next day. He and Ulu were at peace.

The next generation: Kayu.

Late in the summer of 1995, Phil and I decided it was time for a reunion climb. He had acquired a charming Siberian female, Kayu, who was two years old. We had actually met on the Mount Si trail several months before, going in opposite directions, and

Sasha accepted her graciously, although without enthusiasm.

We selected Bandit Mountain, not far from his cabin near Lake Wenatchee, and met on a sunny afternoon at the trailhead to Schaefer Lake. Miss Sasha was a model citizen, staying within 50 feet of us, but always ahead. She judiciously trotted at a moderate pace, and pretty much ignored Woot and Kayu.

Kayu had the enormous energy of an adolescent, and was frequently off to one side of the trail or another, and Woot—her middle-aged suitor—worked hard to keep up with his "trophy bride." She resembles Ulu in having a rather plain white face, but otherwise resembles Sasha in size and configuration, but not in activity. She did not walk at all, but ran everywhere with great enthusiasm.

When we got to Schaefer Lake, Phil urged that we camp higher so as not to disturb the campers there. I was not too happy about climbing farther with a full pack, and was getting a little testy about how high we would have to go to find water this late in the season, but we finally found a modest remnant of old snow near 6000 feet in a draw, and took off our packs.

Only then did we notice that Kayu wasn't with us. Phil reassured me—and himself—that huskies could always find their way, but after a half-hour he walked back down to the start of the draw and whistled and called for her. It was considerably later that she came trotting down from above, with no apologies.

After all had eaten, Kayu wanted to play, and attempted to include Aunt Sasha, but Woot was possessive and aggressively attacked his sister. Sasha had had enough exercise for the day and simply walked away, toward me, for consolation—and protection.

Most of the night, Sasha stayed close by my bivvy bag, and slept, unusual for her at night in the boonies. The other two dogs were rarely around when I occasionally poked my head out. The next morning all three huskies were waiting for Phil and me to get up, and most eager of all was Kayu.

She decided that I deserved first attention, and walked carefully up my bivvy bag and lay down length-wise on me, with her face to mine, generously licking my face. Sasha watched from her spot two or three feet away, with obvious disapproval, evidenced by a soft growl. But soon, all were friends again, and we started out for Bandit Peak.

Bandit has an exceptionally attractive double summit, both of which are steep on all sides. The guide book confesses uncertainty as to "details" of the climb. It suggests going directly up to the ridge west of Schaefer Lake, but examining this long ridge with several other summits and very few level spots, suggests that running this ridge would be a multiday task. We chose to drop down to the level of D Lake, and to traverse low on the north-south ridge. As happened the day before, Sasha led consistently but always within 50 feet, and Kayu with her suitor Woot were frequently out of sight.

After four hours of traversing, we ascended to the shoulder on the north side of Bandit, to discover there was no hope of reaching the west summit, but a reasonable prospect for the east peak. The ridge to the east summit was quite steep, and Phil decided to stay at the shoulder with the three dogs. However, Sasha stayed with me as we tried the ridge top.

After a couple of hundred feet we were confronted with a vertical step that neither of us wanted to descend. Sasha had already decided that a heather ramp on the east side of the ridge looked more promising, and preceded me up it. I caught up with her pacing back and forth before a slab with narrow and intermittent ledges, and only fingertip holds for me. I told her to stay, and climbed onward. Sasha did not vocalize her frustration but explored every other possibility, while I cautiously proceeded to the summit.

Looking back, I saw that Phil had called Sasha and she was briefly with him and the other two huskies. Then she rapidly came back toward the summit, followed by Kayu. I was a little worried about Kayu, although I had long ago learned that Sasha had a definite limit in what she would attempt. This trait is very reassuring to me, permitting me to finish several difficult climbs without seriously endangering Sasha.

Fortunately, Kayu demonstrated the same good judgment, and after personally checking out the route, went back to Phil. I wished that I could share the actual summit with Sasha, but soon all five of us were on our way back to high camp.

While we were packing up our gear, a pilgrim came down the trail. He expressed relief that the dogs were with us. He had spent the previous night camped on the long ridge above us, as suggested by the guide book. (This was his second try, and he confirmed that this route is impossible for a two-day outing.)

As he was eating his supper at his remote site, he believed he was miles from mankind, and even fancied he could hear a distant coyote. Something caught his eye, and there not four inches from his hand was a head that looked *very* wolf-like. He admitted to a rush of adrenaline, but then noticed that the wolf had a blue collar. It was Kayu. The absence from our camp the night before was explained, and we all had a good laugh.

In many ways those two days with Kayu stirred memories of the youthful Sasha, both good and bad. The incredible stamina and unlimited enthusiasm were admirable, but I concluded that I preferred my older Sasha, with her stamina seasoned by reason-ableness and sweetness.

10

❖ THE EXPERT CLIMBER ❖

A New Year's Day ascent.
On January first, a couple of years ago, Sasha and I decided
to take a hike by ourselves on McClellan Butte. I have climbed
this peak with a superficial resemblance to the Matterhorn almost
as many times as Mount Si, since they are both close to Seattle,
and even when the days are very short, a round trip can be accomplished in daylight.

I have a particular fondness for the Butte since my two
younger boys climbed it with me when they were only six and
nine years old in "book time," the time usually required for competent adults to climb a peak listed in Beckey's guide. (My trick
was simple: when they asked for a break, we stopped. As soon as
the first one got up to investigate a pine cone or a bug, we started
up again.) The summit photo from that day remains one of my all-
time favorites, with the highway far below, leading toward Snoqualmie Pass.

This day there was very little snow at the passes, so skiing
was out of the picture, and for the same reason, climbing was possible. It was *not* a nice day, drizzling off and on, with poor visibility, but cold enough for Sasha's taste. We didn't encounter snow
on the ground until we were just a hundred feet or so below the

summit, on the north side. The summit block is steep, with few handholds, requiring caution even in summer. On this dismal day it was the ugliest I have ever seen it: the snow of the previous week had melted and then frozen, and now had a couple of inches of fresh powder on top of the ice.

I thought from inspecting the route that Sasha would decline the summit bid, but to prove the superiority of her 4-wheel drive and built-in crampons, she scrambled up the icy rock as though it were the stairway to our bedroom. Meanwhile, I was inching up very slowly, trying to decide if the ice axe was going to be a help or a hindrance in case of a slip. Twice she came back from the summit to see what I was doing before I finally joined her there.

And a dreadful summit it was, with winds whipping the sleet horizontally, driving particles of ice into our faces, and with a view consisting only of white-on-white. I opted for lunch at the shoulder below, out of the wind, and Sasha would follow a lunch almost anywhere. She soon was in the lead, and out of sight. She came back a couple of times to check on the lunch, and when we got to the final fifty feet at the bottom of the summit block, she literally ran down it, and sat down to wait next to a surprised climber newly arrived—he was very impressed by her nonchalance.

Chaval. A remote fortress.

For some of us, keeping track of the number of peaks we have climbed seems important. The Mountaineers reward this peak-bagging with lapel pins for summitting on the highest volcanic peaks in Washington. The branches in Everett and Tacoma also have a series of handsome peak pins recognizing successful ascents. I had climbed all of the Everett Peaks except one, and although it is not necessary to climb all of the peaks in each group, I held off applying for the pin until I could complete them all. The last obstacle was a peak called Chaval.

Chaval is not a particularly high summit, at 7127 feet. However, it is more remote than it appears when examining the topographic map or the guide book. The standard route crosses a large, old clear cut covered by several years' growth of heavy brush on top of downed logs and stumps, which stopped our first attempt.

Our second attempt was an epic failure. We ascended some old growth timber, traversed above the clear cut, and then encountered a series of the most disagreeable brush-choked basins I have ever experienced. These were from a quarter to a half mile in width at the level we traversed them, up high.

The "nicest" parts were choked with ferns that were chest high, which obscured what was underneath, leading to frequent abrupt drops of a couple of feet or more. The heat was intense, with no shade and not the faintest breeze. The more diabolical parts of these basins were slippery and filled with devil's club and blackberry bushes. A third type of brush was provided by vine maple and slide alder, whose strong limbs initially run close to the ground, down hill, reflecting the weight of winter snow—after two or three feet they rise to meet the sun, intertwining as they ascend.

Traversing cross-grain through this brush with a full pack is genuinely character-building. The incessant resistance to progress through a hundred yards of these is enough to raise serious doubts in the mind of even the most dedicated pilgrim. However, if you quit, you have to go back through it again to get off the mountain! Usually, an unreasonable conviction is formed that if you persist, an alternate route down will be obvious from a higher perspective, allowing one to avoid the green hell on the descent.

On this day in July, we persisted for hours, our sweat attracting pine needles and other plant debris inside our T-shirts to add itching to the range of aesthetic pleasures. We finally exited the last of the brush at seven in the evening. At that point we had "only" to climb a very steep headwall of several hundred feet of wet rocks covered with old pine needles to reach the planned campsite.

Ed declared that he had "flamed out" and didn't want to go any farther. I was not the least upset. Ed had been keeping an eye out for a suitable campsite, and it was not long backtracking until we had pitched his green Gore-tex tent on a small shelf on a minor rib. Although there was no stream, there was old avalanche snow in a nearby gully and we soon had snow melting for water.

Sasha seemed much less tired than Ed or I. She enjoyed a considerable advantage going through the brush. Under the top layer of vegetation the leaves are fewer, permitting her to actually see where she is treading and to avoid at least some of the brambles.

Sasha, as usual, had an entertaining night, stalking something in a cave a hundred feet above our tent, but for some reason she did not explore laterally to eat snow. (I am convinced that dogs cannot smell water or snow and depend on visual identification.) When morning came she made it clear that she was quite thirsty.

After a guided tour over to the snow for Sasha's sake, we packed up and headed back into the green hell. At least, this time it was morning and cooler, but otherwise no more pleasant than the day before.

This wasn't the first peak to require three attempts for us, but I can't think of any peak that had been more tediously unpleasant. (Mount Garfield had been seriously life-threatening, but never tedious). Back in Seattle, we made a few calls and found two people who had successfully climbed Chaval. Dan had gone the way we did, but had done it in early spring, with the help of snow cover. He had descended the tributary of Illabot Creek in the black of night, suggesting that his appetite for suffering and risk-taking made his route selection suspect. Silas had gone up the ridge all the way, a route that was a couple of miles longer, but as we found, infinitely more pleasant.

We tried Silas' route later that month, this time driving up and camping by the car for an early start. The next day we reached a divide by noon, and had pitched our tent by 2pm. After exploring an alternate route, we decided to drop down a few hundred feet from the ridge at the divide where we had stopped for lunch, even though we couldn't see all of that route; the major problem on that route would be finding an exit from the rock onto the glacier.

We returned to camp, relatively fresh and optimistic. Although we had elected to put up our tent on snow, since that was the most level spot, Sasha slept—what little she did—on a bare spot on the ground.

Up at five the next morning, we packed, descended to the divide, and dropped everything but summit packs. We lost at least a half-hour trying to avoid losing altitude by traversing on rock, which led to some Class 4 climbing, unroped. I finally was able to descend to the glacier; Ed decided that my route was unacceptable, and Sasha followed Ed as he backtracked for a few hundred feet and gained the glacier at a level only a hundred feet lower than my route. At this point Ed gave up and found a dry spot to watch from.

Sasha caught up with me while I was putting on crampons, and soon was literally several hundred feet above me on the steep snow. In general, she keeps close enough to maintain visual contact with me. On a trail, that means that she will hold up until I round the bend into her field of vision, but on the huge glacier below Chaval she was able to extend her lead to nearly a half-mile.

Although there were no tracks, she could see the summit area and chose a contoured route, remaining in the lead all the way. We had our usual summit reunion, and much to my surprise, it had taken us only three hours from the divide. Although Sasha was sure that it was lunch time, it was only mid-morning, so we began our descent.

At this point in a climb, it is predictable that Sasha will rush back to Ed, to see if he is okay, and if he has any food that he doesn't want to carry back. Chaval was no exception, and consequently, Sasha climbed it one and a half times, because she then returned back up the glacier to guide me back.

The sun had been blocked by high clouds that morning, and the down-draft off the glacier was chilling, but by noon, the late July sun had burned through and warmed up everything. The long, west-running ridge was free of snow and water after the first hundred feet and the temperature rose inexorably during the five and a half hours of descent. Sasha had been a great help finding our tracks, but we lost her during the last hour. She was thirsty, and knew there was water near the car in the form of Illabot Creek, good to drink and good for swimming!

Her ability to locate her position in trackless forest is incredible. She not only takes her gift for granted, she assumes that we also have this skill. I have not found a way to convey to her that we lack the ability to find our ascent route, or the car, by smell.

She is most apt to go ahead without waiting for us when she senses the proximity of the car or camp; if I can guess that proximity and call her back, she will remain with us, but if I don't realize it, she will have gone out of earshot. On this day, Ed and I would have appreciated every step saved, but we had to stumble out on our own, to find an only slightly apologetic pup, thoroughly wet and cool, lying in the shade of the wagon.

The walls of the remote fortress had been overcome on this third assault by a pup who was more interested in the climb than in the success—she probably didn't even care about the handsome pin I received that fall from the Everett club.

The winter of 1990-91.

The winter of 1990-91 proved to be a terrible winter for skiing, except for December, which produced one of the heaviest and most enduring snowfalls in Seattle's history. Travel by automobile was so slow that I actually skied in to work on the first day after the storm. It was not a very productive day, since the seven and a half miles required two and a half hours, each way, and Sasha couldn't come.

After this prolonged cold spell there was no snow for weeks, at least at altitudes that encompassed the commercial ski areas and most logging roads, and we turned to climbing again. On short winter days the close-in peaks along Interstate 90 toward Snoqualmie Pass are attractive because of their proximity to Seattle, and some of them have short access roads.

Road 9030 is such a road, which takes off at about 2000 feet elevation and leads to a four-mile trail to Mason Lake. This winter we were able to drive to the trailhead. In spite of a late start, we were soon at Mason Lake, which was at snow level, and we continued up the ridge to Mount Defiance. Ed lagged behind; consequently, Sasha and I were considerably ahead of him as we punched holes in the snow across the broad southern slope below the summit.

The trail gains only a little as it continues from east to west, to reach the western ridge of Defiance. At that point, it turns back uphill on the relatively gentle west ridge to the summit. We had seen no tracks in the fresh snow on the ridge top, and it was a surprise to find another pilgrim already on the summit, who had ap-

96

Sasha on the summit of Mount Defiance, looking downhill toward Ed. Warren is in his polypropylene shirt. (Photo by anonymous peak-bagger).

proached it directly from the east. He was even more surprised, since Sasha, as is her custom, was well in advance of me.

The winter sun was low in the southern sky causing the fresh snow to literally sparkle, and I prevailed on this other peak-bagger to record the scene. He caught Sasha staring intently down the southern slope. (Three years later, on Hidden Lake Peak Trail, I reencountered our photographer. Neither of us recognized each other, but he recognized Sasha and asked to take our picture with his camera, since he had told many of his friends about this beautiful husky he had met on a summit in midwinter.)

It was only later that I found that Ed had left the trail at a point well before we had, and was laboring up that slope in the trees far below us. This is her watchdog pose, which informs any observant human that something of interest is the object of her concentration. When we started down, I chose to plunge-step down that slope, and Sasha quickly disappeared, intercepting Ed lower down, and I never did see him until we met at the lake.

A couple of weeks later we were back on the other side of I-90, looking for some pinnacles that stand on the north flank of Mount Washington. For years Ed and I had looked up at these pinnacles as we drove toward Snoqualmie Pass, swearing that some day we would figure out the approach.

Earlier that fall we had climbed Mount Washington with Rüdiger, following the route description in one of the *100 Hikes* books of Harvey Manning. The trail, an old logging road mostly grown over, doubles back away from the gendarmes, reaching the east side of an intervening ridge, and then heads south on a re-markable connecting ridge called "the great wall of China," which has a flat top almost 30 feet wide, with steep sides extending down at least five hundred feet.

We lunched on the summit of Mount Washington in almost spring-like sunshine, with the ever-present Mount Rainier filling the southern view. We descended in the direction of the pinnacles. It was not really a reasonable approach, as Rüdiger later pointed out, but I finally got close enough to these reddish, granitic gen-darmes to see that they were steep enough to require a rope and hardware for safe climbing.

When we returned in January, Rüdiger had returned to medi-cal school in Hannover, so it was Ed, Sasha and I who returned with a rope on another bright and sunny day, with even less snow. Ed still was nursing the effects of bronchitis and had dropped be-hind. Sasha arrived first at the col between two of the pinnacles. She was whining softly when I joined her, a sound so quiet and high-pitched that you have to be listening for it in order to hear it. I attributed her behavior to mild anxiety about the exposure, a falloff of 75 feet or more, and the narrowness of the ledges.

I offered verbal reassurance, and proceeded to climb up the southerly pinnacle with relative comfort. As I scanned the pan-orama, it became clear that Sasha's complaint was only frustration, and not fear. She had found her way up the first pinnacle that I had not yet attempted, and stood calmly looking down toward Ed.

For five years she had raced me to the summit of simple peaks such as Mount Defiance, clearly demonstrating her under-standing of the goal of our outings. But I had never known her to climb such an exposed and relatively difficult pitch on her own. So much for anxiety.

Descent from Kaleetan.

Last spring, Ed, Sasha and I decided to climb this mountain with a spectacular snow field on its southern flank that persists for much of the summer. As we hiked up the trail to Lake Malakwa (allegedly meaning mosquito), Ed and I needed our ice axes, and Sasha her claws. As the trail crossed over a pass, there were myriad tracks in every direction, none of them concentrated enough to identify the main trail to the lake.

The relatively warm, cloudy day and the deep snow pack caused a thick fog that limited visibility to only a few feet. Consequently we met a number of parties wandering around in the trees, none of whom really knew where the lake was. That may seem improvident, since a contour map and a compass could decide the issue, but that area is so frequently visited by us in the summer when the trail is bare that we hadn't dug out our quadrangle map for this trip, although we had our compasses among our "ten essentials" that we always carried.

Sasha had no idea where we wanted to go. If we had been going back to the car, she would have been well in the lead, with no hesitation, but here she stayed close by, waiting for us to make up our minds.

After a half-hour of wandering we finally emerged from the heavy trees on the southeast side of the lake, with the couloir to Bryant Peak on our right and the long valley ahead of us that leads toward the pass between Kaleetan and Chair Peak. Ed stayed at the lake and Sasha and I had lunch on a small knoll looking down on Lake Malakwa.

As we began lunch, three climbers plodded by, two hundred feet below us. Sasha and I used their steps subsequently as we started up the steep slope on the east side of our objective. They were making good time, and we didn't catch up with them until we reached the southern ridge on Kaleetan. I was pleasantly surprised to find that two of them had been in the climbing class that Ed and I had taught at the University in the late '60s. (The course

Sasha on a pinnacle on Mount Washington. The falloff on the other side is at least 75 feet.

was the same one that had taught us. It later was a casualty of the economics of the insurance industry—the University couldn't obtain liability insurance for the course.)

The disadvantage of this reunion was that I felt obliged to kick the steps all the rest of the way to the summit, on that long south ridge. The fog layer was far below the summit, and although the sky was pearl gray we had a clear view all the way back to the lake.

As we rested on the summit, a couple from the other party ex-

100

pressed concern about the steepness of the snow we had ascended from the valley, and suggested that we continue down the southern ridge to a major gully system that was several hundred feet farther south, which appeared to be less steep. Sasha was puzzled when we went by our up-tracks, and as is her usual communication in that situation, returned and waited a little behind us, to let us know that this was *not* the way down and that she could not be responsible if we went that way.

By the time we reached the couloir we had chosen from our summit view, Sasha was again in the lead, and had investigated it thoroughly before the four people arrived. She didn't think much of our choice. There was a cornice about six feet above a small ledge which supported a small fir tree; this ledge connected to a series of narrow ledges that allowed a sloping—and slippery— traverse to our left. There were at least a hundred feet of bare rock before the continuous snow of the couloir led to the bottom of the valley 500 feet below.

I stomped one step a couple of feet down from the lip of the cornice, but the cornice was overhung; it was possible for a person to back down, holding onto an ice axe planted into the snow on top. However, there was no simple solution for Sasha, and she refused to go before or after me. I was convinced that she would not have major difficulty, and would not go far if she slipped.

After several minutes of encouragement, she still would not attempt the cornice. I told her to "go around," which is a command that sometimes causes her to go back the way she had come, and indeed she would disappear for a few minutes, but then she would reappear at the cornice, complaining loudly about being abandoned.

I finally went on down the snow, planning to go to the valley bottom and then retrace our original route, and call her back up to that point. I began my turn northward, and told the other three not to wait since it might take as much as an hour. Consequently they were several hundred vertical feet below me when I saw Sasha come running down the snow below the cornice.

I am not sure how she managed to get off the cornice, but I am sure that she was angry at me. Although I called to her and she briefly glanced my way, she headed straight for the other three, with whom she stayed until I finally caught up at the lake. She was *not* a happy camper, but she had again shown a remarkable ability to solve problems and survive! She forgave me, but only after half a candy bar.

A belay for Sasha on Thunder Mountain.

Before Sasha had joined our climbing team, on a spring weekend, Ed and I had slogged on snow up to Surprise Lake. Our objective was Thunder Mountain. The guide book described a walkup on the western ridge that extends up from the second lake; consequently we had brought no rope or technical equipment, only our ice axes.

After a couple of hours on moderately steep, soft snow we came to the summit block, towering several hundred feet over us, consisting of steep, broken steps with scattered evergreens. We were surprised by its vertical nature, to say the least. Ed announced that "it wasn't worth it," an unarguable statement, but he agreed that I could proceed with him waiting at the bottom, as a "support party."

I scrambled up until I arrived at a completely vertical face that appeared to be only 30 feet in height, which I estimated would end on the false summit. There were a couple of crack systems that I was confident could be climbed if I had a rope and some hardware for protection. I reluctantly descended, grumbling at the route description, but I began planning a return with proper equipment.

This next summer my son Karl agreed to attempt a first ascent of this face route on Thunder Mountain. We got a late start on Saturday afternoon, and it was quite dark when we set up our tent at Glacier Lake. As we started to prepare our dinner by flashlight, we discovered that I had left Sasha's dinner and her next day's lunch at home in the fridge, along with my lunch for the next day. It was already at least three hours after Sasha's usual dinner time, and she was more intense than usual with her "death stare."

Fortunately, I had brought an extra freeze-dried dinner for Karl, and he didn't need it, so I gave Sasha half of that relatively expensive dish, and saved the other half for her breakfast, in lieu of a lunch. She didn't seem all that impressed with the gourmet meal, but she sensed that the new cuisine was going to be the only choice, and quickly downed it.

We arose at dawn and started up the ridge, which was much less pleasant than when it was covered with snow. At the summit block, Sasha was anxious because she found no obvious way higher. I put her on "stay," as Karl and I started up. Although we didn't get out the rope at that point, Karl complained that this was clearly Class 4 climbing.

After a couple of hundred feet upward, I found a suitable place for a belay, just below a pillar. Around the pillar and up, there was the ledge that I had explored a year earlier. We put on our climbing harnesses and I got out my rack of Friends and chocks, and put my hand into one of the cracks for a jam hold. It had been raining for most of that week, and although the rock looked dry, the inside of the crack was lined with soft lichen which was quite wet. Not only could I not get my hand to stay in, I couldn't persuade the cams of the Friend to stay in. I pulled the Friend out twice with very little effort, a sobering event. I realized, after half an hour of trying alternatives, that I was again stymied by this mountain.

At about this time I heard Karl talking earnestly with someone, but I couldn't hear the responses. I inched over toward the edge of the pillar and looked down to see that the newcomer was Sasha. Since Karl had complained about the difficulty more than once on our ascent, we were both amazed at her achievement, a sentiment followed quickly by concern for how we would get her back down.

Karl is an engineer and a good person to have along when creating a belay harness for a dog. Sasha showed no enthusiasm for the project, but did not resist, and soon was securely in a harness of one inch nylon webbing. We decided that Sasha would be tied to my harness by a short runner from her harness. I attached my rappel ring to the paired climbing ropes, which were secured around a sturdy cedar, and started down with Sasha in the lead.

One problem was immediately apparent. On her way up Sasha had gone under several low branches that I could not get under, but she saw no reason not to descend the same way, which meant some complicated unhitching and rehitching as we descended. I marveled at her route. Unfortunately, the paired 165 foot ropes reached only to the crux of the climb, which was still 50 feet away from the base, which meant we had to proceed with no belay or rappel, with Sasha still tied to me.

In retrospect, I should have untied her, since if she fell, there was a good chance that I would not be able to prevent both of us from falling. She didn't seem alarmed, since she was familiar with her route, but she did proceed with obvious caution as we both inched down, I holding onto the rock, and she leading ever-so-gently until we were down. The ordeal didn't affect her appetite, and she was able to con me out of half of my meager lunch.

Bald Mountain: huckleberries and a vertical climb.

In search of a summit we had not climbed within a reasonable drive from Seattle, Ed and I decided to try the southern approach to Marble Pass, used around the turn of the century as an approach to mines in the Sultan Basin from the village of Silverton on the southern branch of the Mountain Loop Highway.

We had tried to find the northern approach several months earlier without success—lower altitude trails are quickly overgrown in western Washington, and even old roads. This day we were able to find the beginning of the old road, which was drivable only for a half-mile. Not only did we not find the trail, we had considerable difficulty following the remnants of the logging road. After a full morning of bashing about, we had made precious little progress. We gave up and went back to the car for lunch.

Plan B for that day was Bald Mountain, also in the Sultan basin, which had the advantage of a maintained trail. Actually, the road was blocked some way before the trailhead, and much of the road and lower trail were in ugly clear cuts. It was not turning out to be an aesthetic day, and I was increasingly thinking about returning to the car, when we abruptly reached the ridge top.

It was as beautiful as the earlier part of the scenery was depressing. On the north side of the ridge were dark alpine fir and hemlock, well spaced in lush green meadows. The rock was granitic, and it was so light hued that it looked like snow in places. Farther down on the north side were two small, dark blue lakes whose ripples from the wind were visible from the pass only as a satin texture. One-half mile farther along the ridge was the summit of Bald Mountain, rising like a cathedral, with nearly vertical walls on all sides, and a gable.

Ed had lagged behind, being less motivated to summit, but I felt a strong need to stand on top of this very attractive peak. I hiked quickly along the ridge, hoping that on the other side there would be an approach that was less vertical, but with a climber's ambivalence hoped that the ascent would not be too easy!

The trail completely circled this summit block, and then headed down, never actually approaching it closer than 100 feet. Finding nothing encouraging on the downhill side, we reversed, and left the trail on the west ridge to the cathedral. I walked straight ahead, although I could see nothing but an "open book" that lay back only 10 to 20 degrees from the vertical.

There was a small ledge half way up, and Sasha quickly scrambled up to that. When I arrived at the ledge, Sasha was pacing back and forth, whining very softly, which I now understand as a sign of frustration, not fear. I dismissed the thought that she could climb any higher, and as I stepped around her to the start of the next pitch, I assured her that I would be back quickly, and that she should "stay."

Sasha had plans of her own—she scrambled between my legs, and started up this nearly vertical open book. There were one or two small patches of moss and grass in the crack, only an inch or so in width, that she sunk her claws into as she scrambled up until she was at least 10 feet directly above my head. She ran out of momentum at that point and I was suddenly confronted with the likelihood of a 50 pound dog falling on me, where I stood on this small ledge, 30 feet above the broken rock at the base.

The pause seemed a very long one, and she glanced down for a second, considering the alternatives. Then she gave a tremendous leap, got her forelegs on the lip of the vertical section and mantled up and away, with scrambling rear feet.

I can't say whether the relief I felt was greater than the elation for her accomplishment, but I was exceptionally proud of my athlete. This emotion was followed within seconds by the realization that there was no way that I could persuade her to come back down that way, which had appeared to be easier than any other I had seen when I had walked around the summit block.

When I quickly joined her on the summit, she was calmly examining the view of Spada Reservoir, like a mountain goat. After sharing a candy bar, she began exploring for an exit. She easily managed a steep traverse on a slab that was quite uncomfortable for me, since there were no handholds and was dangerously exposed—lost footing would have ended on rocks a painful distance below. Then she suddenly became conservative, and waited for me to find the next section. She didn't think much of my lead, but she hesitated only a moment and we were soon back at the base.

On the trail back, I rounded a corner and found her with her head in the low bushes at the side of the trail. This was unusual for her, since she is reluctant to surrender the lead when she is confident of the route. I shortly realized that she was picking huckleberries, quite selectively, using the precision of her lips and teeth to avoid the leaves. I had not even noticed the berries, but we then both browsed our way, traversing the north side of the ridge, before dropping back onto the south side.

After a mile or so, I noticed that I hadn't seen Sasha for a while, and concluded that she had gone on ahead to catch Ed. However, she returned sooner than expected, and was content to stay close to me for the next half-mile.

Then I saw the problem. A man with a huge samoyed was just ahead on the trail, and Sasha was unable to pass peacefully. The master was unaware of the drama at his back, but I saw the same sequence played out three times.

As Sasha approached, the large dog quietly turned sideways in the trail and made it clear that his duty was to prevent Sasha from getting too close to his master. Sasha seemed to understand, and each time would stop and turn away, to inspect something a few feet off the trail.

The large dog would then look relieved and a little apologetic, and his hind legs would quiver as he ran to catch up with his master. Finally, I spoke to the samoyed and his master acknowledged us, and stepped aside. Everyone was relieved, most of all, the samoyed.

I drove home with the conviction that Sasha was not only the best canine rock climber in the world, but sensitive to the needs of others!

Goat Island Mountain and the goats.

One fall day, before the snow but in that worrisome time after hunting season has opened, Ed, Sasha and I decided upon Goat Island Mountain. I confess I didn't even think about the name of this long, high ridge that runs for some miles off the side of Mount Rainier.

The approach is scenic, about three miles of trail along small, fast-flowing rivers, but then it was cross-country and up nearly two thousand feet of moderately steep forest. After that there was almost a thousand feet of grassland and then desolate rubble fields. The summit was over 7000 feet high and had only a few small, desperate-looking alpine cedars and fir, at the very limit of vegetation. On this clear fall day Mount Rainier—Tahoma, as it rightly should be called—filled the entire western horizon, and to the south, Little Tahoma, Wonderland, and the Cowlitz Chimneys completed the panorama.

On the way up, Sasha was never out of my sight for more than a few seconds. When we got close to the summit, though, I lost sight of her. That is not unusual for her, whose competitive spirit is particularly obvious near any summit. However, I was surprised when I got to the barren summit to find no wolf-dog. I called her by whistling several times, and still I could see nothing of her.

As I sat down on a rock for lunch, I heard the sound of a bleating goat, and looked over toward the origin of the ridge from Tahoma. There a herd of seven goats, including two little ones, were descending into the basin to the north. The sound of rolling and sliding rocks testified to the steepness. I continued to watch their progress, until I saw Sasha trotting slowly up the ridge from the direction of the goats. I assumed that she had only wanted a closer look.

In retrospect, she may have been a little subdued when she re-joined me, although she ate her lunch with no hesitation. On the way down, we took a "short cut" and as usual, she stayed close behind or only slightly in front, since my return route was not her choice. Back at the car, she jumped in quickly and lay down in the back of Ed's Tercel. She remained quiet all the way back home, but that was not unusual for a dog that is as attentive to rest after exertion as she is to food when hungry.

The ride was a little over two hours, enough for all of us to get a little stiff, and when we opened up the rear of the car at home, Sasha made no effort to get up. I pulled her cushion forward a little to encourage her, and she screamed.

That got my attention and I discovered blood on the pad she sleeps on, and a gaping wound about three inches in length on her left inner thigh. It was no longer bleeding, and looked as though it had been cut by a scalpel. It was quite clean after what must have been a thorough cleaning by her tongue.

Ordinarily, Sasha would prefer almost anything rather than be-ing picked up, but she had no reservations this time about my gently picking her up and placing her on her feet on the driveway. Still, she wouldn't walk. I again picked her up and carried her up-stairs to the family room where she lay exactly as I had placed her, with a distinct air of martyrdom.

Ellie was back East, and I had to make a lonely decision about what to do next. I decided on first things first. I prepared Sasha's usual dinner and brought it to her side. With elaborate histrionics she raised her head and ate every bite, without once rolling over on her stomach. Similarly, she had a long drink of water, and laid her head back down with a sigh, as though it might be her last act.

After I unpacked, warmed up and ate a TV dinner, she began to whine. I was anxious, and considered calling the vet, although I had already decided that I didn't want the wound sutured, out of concern for sewing up germs in the wound. She continued to whine, and I guessed that she wanted to potty, so I picked her up and struggled downstairs with her, hoping not to trip on anything. I deposited her near her customary spot, just off the turnaround and she immediately emptied her bladder.

Then, she forgot her terminal condition and executed a little sideways leap back onto the tarmac, one of her patented moves designed to avoid stepping in something. She looked surprised that all of her parts worked, stood for a second, and then confidently trotted back upstairs into the house, and refused to discuss the matter any further. As far as she was concerned, she was now fully recovered.

In considering the events of that day, the only scenario that makes sense was that Sasha got too close to one of the kids, and one of the older goats gored her. Their horns are wickedly sharp and relatively narrow, about 10 inches in length, and nearly vertical. I can't imagine any other way that Sasha could get an incision on the inside of her thigh, and since I hadn't heard her yelp when she sustained the wound, it must have occurred when she was away from me, checking out the goats.

Sasha isn't talking about the incident, but the next encounter with a momma goat with her kid established that she *had* learned how dangerous these goats can be.

It was last summer when we climbed Sloan Peak. We had exited the glacier on the east side of the mountain and were ascending a steep section of trail on the south side. Sasha was nearly a hundred yards ahead of me, and I had just told her that she was a smart-ass, when she turned toward me and trotted leisurely back down the trail.

I was surprised that she took my message so to heart, but then the source of this new obedience emerged around the corner in the person of a very large momma goat with a yearling close behind. Momma was indignant and intent on teaching Sasha a lesson, but Sasha, a quick learner, didn't need another lesson. Still, her dignity required that she not run away from the self-appointed teacher, so the goat was actually gaining on her as they both descended the trail toward me.

I finally spoke to the momma goat, pointing out that my ice axe was at least as long as her horns, and that she should mind her own business. She slowed, and finally stopped, and did not move for several minutes. I immediately took off my pack and began taking pictures each 10 feet as I slowly approached her—Sasha had found something behind me that required her presence. I had taken only three shots before momma decided that we weren't good students anyway, and led her kid straight up a granitic ledge, stopping once more to remind Sasha of her manners. Sasha needed no reminder. Her courage was intact, and we finished the relatively difficult cork-screw ascent of this beautiful mountain without further hesitation.

Sasha the problem solver.

From the first, Sasha made many decisions on her own, such as deciding to find me on our early climb of Mount Thompson. Many problems had to be solved, but most had fairly direct solutions such as walking around a boulder field instead of directly across it. At home, her two- and three-part charades gave strong evidence of her reasoning ability and her ability to solve problems. But her ability to solve problems in the mountains was made particularly clear last summer when we climbed Bedal Peak.

She and I were ascending the east ridge, above the lake, when I came to a notch with a 30 foot cliff that was nearly vertical. I knew that the conservative response was to backtrack a quarter-mile to a more gentle notch that could be descended to the gentler slopes on the south side, to bypass the difficult notch. On the other hand, I was tired, and the cliff had good hand and foot holds, and I chose to downclimb it. Sasha did not complain, as she certainly would have when she was younger. Instead, she carefully searched every inch of the ledge she was on to look for a way down.

Several times she frightened me by actually starting down my route, but there was no way that it could be done without hands. I yelled each time, "Sasha, NO!" and she would back up and search again. I then commanded, "Sasha, go around," a phrase she had more or less mastered in relation to our back lot, when her rope became caught around a tree.

Several times she started back the way we had come, but she found nothing to her liking in a short distance, and returned to the ledge. I finally resumed climbing, but would frequently turn around and repeat the command, signaling with my hand to go back. The problem was a difficult one because it was a short distance to her objective, me, but not a safe distance.

The solution required her to turn away from her objective, and go back a quarter-mile and descend where neither of us had gone before. I was delighted when I next saw her, now on the south slope, at a trot toward me. It was literally only five minutes before she had passed me, back on the ridge, without acknowledging my praise.

The rest of the ascent was simple drudgery, but successful. (I think it was Rébuffat who said that climbing consisted of hours of tedium and seconds of sheer terror.) But on the descent, as we followed an animal trail down the ridge, I noticed that we were below the altitude where we had gained the ridge crest, and I realized that Sasha had decided not to return the way we had come, but to take a shortcut back to the Sloan Creek Trail.

I debated with myself whether I should trust her judgment and follow her or not—but my 30 years of climbing argued that shortcuts are rarely that, but usually mean more work than sticking to the ascent route. Sasha did not mind when I whistled her back and we commenced a long traverse back to our original route. As we regained the route, and I observed the ridge she had chosen to descend, there was no question it would have gone easily, and substantially shorter than our original route.

Thinking back, I am confident now that there were several times before that she had tried to help by directing me in a somewhat different way back. We humans are slow learners!

Sasha and mountain weather.

Huskies are probably better prepared for mountain weather than are most dogs. The major exception is heat. It doesn't help that her coat is solid black on top; if you pat her ruff when she is in the sun, it is definitely warm. She pants efficiently, but uses a large amount of water in the process of cooling herself in this manner. In fact, she drinks the same amount as I although I weigh three times as much.

To Sasha, water is not just for drinking. She takes advantage of every opportunity to wet her feet, and in warm weather, her legs and belly if possible. Recently, Ed and I had split at a trail junction. I climbed to the summit of Mastiff Peak and Ed took the rightward trail to Merritt Lake a half-mile away. There was no water on my route and I shared my water with her, but after the summit she left me to run down the trail to catch Ed. At the trail junction, she smelled Ed's tracks toward the lake, and took off in that direction.

A troop of Boy Scouts was camped at the lake, and reported later that she trotted up and searched unsuccessfully for Ed who had come and gone back down. Confident that her own speed and endurance would allow her to catch up with him, she waded into the lake, drinking and swimming laps as she cooled off. The troop apparently cheered, but soon she was off again, and beat me back to the junction.

Summer nights—and days, for that matter—can be a problem other than heat. Rain has never bothered her when we are in the mountains, although at home, she sometimes behaves as though she might die if she got any rain on her thick coat. But in the mountains, she has never asked to come into the tent with Ed and me at night. Except once!

We were camped on a high ridge near Glacier Peak, and a storm moved through during the night that was as spectacular for its lightning as I can remember. When it first began to light up the walls of the tent, I expected her to want to come in with us, and Ed would have agreed. But she must have been some distance away, because by the time it had started to rain heavily and she asked to come in she was soaked, and Ed said "no way."

I tried to reassure her through the tent wall, and she finally left, perhaps to find the cover of a tree. I felt badly about failing her in her hour of need, but I was confident of her ability to survive the thunder and lightning. Indeed she was close by when dawn came, and didn't seem upset with us.

Later that same year, in early October, we had camped at a high lake at 6000 feet, and it soon became obvious that it would be a very cold night. I watched her select a site, circling round and round, with her peculiar trance-like head bobbing, followed by lying down in a tight circle with her tail over her nose. When we arose the next morning, all the ground was frosted with the exception of a single circle near our tent. Sasha, on the other hand, was coated with a thin film of frost on her back, a clear demonstration of the insulating property of her coat.

Her insulation would undoubtedly be even better if we did not let her sleep indoors with us every night. We don't regret it, and we know she prefers to sleep with us, since she can—and does, occasionally—go outside at night through her pet door, but never stays out.

Sasha versus the radical conservationists.

Having been a card-carrying member of several organizations that are either conservationists, or climbing and hiking groups that secondarily support conservation causes, I was annoyed to find some leaders of these organizations lobbying the Forest Service to declare Wilderness Areas off-limits to dogs. Even worse, some want to declare almost any mountain a Wilderness. They have actually claimed that Mount Si, an "outdoor gym" for many of us for conditioning, was a Wilderness complete with grizzly bears!

The Mountaineers Club leadership never held a referendum on the subject, but simply concluded that dogs were "incompatible" with the Wilderness. Curiously, they didn't argue that horses, weighing 40 times more and shod with steel, should be excluded. Come to that, damage to trails or off-trail terrain by two legged people weighing 150 pounds, shod in stiff boots, greatly exceeds the damage by a four-legged dog weighing 50 pounds (75 pounds per impact versus 12.5). Even worse, they didn't argue that hunting is incompatible.

Some complain about bad behavior of dogs—in or out of the Wilderness—and with grounds. Sasha has been attacked at least three times by unsocialized dogs, and I felt great anger, particularly when they broke skin. But surely the answer is to condemn and punish owners who irresponsibly take unrestrained and anti-social animals out, just as we condemn human offenders as individuals, and not as an entire race or gender.

As one who values the health benefits of vigorous and sustained exercise, I wish to share these benefits with my dog. Her

113

companionship in the mountains, which we both love, is important to us both. I will resist efforts by anti-dog and anti-use zealots, and continue to assert my historical rights, and as a taxpayer, to climb with my well-behaved Sasha.

11

❖ THE PRINCESS ❖

The adoration of a dog by her owners, particularly "grand-parents" who have raised their family and can afford more affection for a pet in their dotage, may be regarded as excessive by (a) those who would never regard a pet as of great importance, or (b) those who are still preoccupied with real children.

On the other hand, these excesses are very understandable to people caught in the same close bond with their own pet. In fact, it is amusing to see the relief expressed by others when you reveal this deep affection you feel for your dog. The conversation then turns into a long and spirited exchange of anecdotes about each other's critters, boring to others, although similar in effect to doting grandparents exchanging pictures of their latest grandchild with other grandparents.

Worst of all must be listening to two owners of Siberian huskies comparing the ways of their pups. For example, Ellie and I regularly sit around the table after meals and discuss the grace and beauty of our princess.

Sasha's cat-like posture when she is lying down almost always gets our attention, even after years of wondering how she manages it. We know how she enters into the position: she simply sits down on her haunches and pushes back over her rear legs as she lies down. Her rear feet end up sticking almost straight in front, just an inch or so outside her elbows. Her thighs are folded under her, which probably has an advantage for insulation in the arctic. (Most dogs lie with their rear legs more squarely under their body.) Whether it is due to this cat-like posture, or in spite of it, Sasha can spring straight into the air from this position to a height of several feet. This posture reflects her unique lightfootedness, and her powerful legs, not to mention her grace.

Sasha sits in this position for hours when she is on our deck, watching the neighborhood. She took advantage of our picnic table, which reaches the top of the solid railing around the deck, sitting with her paws hanging over the railing. When winter came, and the picnic table was stored in the garage, she seemed much less content to stay on the deck.

Happily, Ellie's dad took up woodcraft in his retirement, and one of his most successful products at senior center sales was a child-size picnic table. Grandpa Haglund had no trouble making a table just for Sasha, that could stay out all year long. Now, Sasha can always keep an eye on the neighborhood, although occasionally she has to stand on her hind legs to peer over another part of the deck railing, whereas Tioga and Nootka are tall enough to simply peer out, standing on all four feet.

As she sits on the deck, she appears to be an alert watchdog. God knows she *is* alert; she even watches birds and jets flying over, and knows where most of the neighborhood squirrels are at any time. On the other hand, she almost never barks. It is possible that this is effective in the function of a watchdog, since a burglar might conclude that she *wanted* him to come inside the fence, in the manner of Sylvia's "watchdogs from Hell."

Communications.

Like most people owned by their pet, there are many "conversations," with both sides of the conversation provided by Ellie or me. However, there are also conversations that she initiates.

When she and I have been sharing the study quietly for some time, she may decide that it is time for a break. She sits in her cat stance, pointing straight at me, and then begins a series of vocal-

Sasha sitting in her silly position on her very own table, made by Grandpa Haglund. This table allows her to look out from her deck without standing up on her hind legs. (Photo by Ellie Guntheroth).

izations, punctuated by little forward punches of both forefeet. These vocalizations are somewhere between a bark and a short howl, and they have a predictable pattern for a given subject. Katie, who has studied on this, feels she can accurately interpret specific messages from her Tioga and Nootka.

I am less attuned to these nuances, but there are times when the message is unmistakable. At four o'clock on a Sunday afternoon when we are both home, the message is simply, "I'm hungry and I would like you to make my dinner."

At other times, the message is, "It's play time and I want your undivided attention." She even talked to the cat at times, attempting to persuade Snidely to chase her. Sometimes it worked, and after a brief vocalization, Sasha could be heard running desperately around the house, sliding around corners, to escape the dreaded feline. However, Snidely never really figured out what to do with a 50 pound husky if he had ever caught her, so the game was usually brief.

There is no doubt whatsoever that Sasha was jealous of Snidely the cat. On many evenings Sasha would wait to eat her food until she determined what else was available; unfortunately, this meant that Snidely had an opportunity to check Sasha's dish, and to eat the fresh meat part, leaving the dried pellets. This invariably galvanized Sasha, and she would scare away the cat and scarf down her dinner.

Her jealousy was not confined to the cat. Although she doesn't particularly like to be petted, Tioga and Nootka do, and get a good deal of that from Katie and Karl. When they stay at our house for a few days while their folks are away, they come to Ellie or me for their ration of affection. Sasha watches, and after a while also presents herself for her share.

She has shown just a bit of jealousy of our grandchildren Callie Grace and Peter. Fortunately, Karl is thoughtful enough to take time to give Sasha some undivided attention when they visit us. He gets down on the floor and presents his beard for Sasha, which she is unusually fond of.

He also involves Sasha when he is walking around the house entertaining one of the children, occasionally pretending that they are airplanes, strafing the doggies. Both the children and Sasha begin to vocalize as they get caught up in the game.

Callie, as the first grandchild, is a princess in her own right, and is probably the only creature in this world that can compete with Sasha for our attention, and win. At least, that was true until Peter came, and although he hasn't replaced Callie, he has captured his full "market share."

Both of them have been at ease with Sasha since the beginning, thanks in no small part to their own big doggies. Compared to the bulk of Nootka and Tioga, Sasha is not the least intimidating—on the contrary, the children enjoyed terrorizing Sasha. One

Sasha looking over the railing from the deck, with Nootka on her immediate right, and Tioga barely visible.

of their more charming methods is to growl at Sasha, something I presume Nootka taught them. (They both could growl before they could say Mama).

Occasionally, Sasha has to retreat behind the couch, but she rarely leaves the area where they are playing or napping, suggesting that she enjoys their company in spite of their behavior. Nevertheless, like grandparents, Sasha prefers brief visits to their house, and nowadays makes it clear to Ellie and me that she is ready to go home as soon as we are. That is understandable for a house with two adults, two very active children, two large dogs, and two cats.

Before Peter was born, Sasha and Callie took turns entertaining one another. Sasha began the exchanges when Callie hadn't yet learned to walk and was lying on her sheepskin in the middle of the family room floor. Sasha walked over to the small cardboard box that contains her toys: a two-foot piece of old climbing rope, two tennis balls, and a peculiar black cylinder that resembles a toilet tank device that, when thrown, has an extremely elusive bounce. Sasha usually noses through her collection and selects one to bring to us for a game.

On this occasion, she picked up the entire box without spilling any toys, and walked over to Callie's sheepskin and gently dumped the contents in front of her. At other times, Callie would select a toy for Sasha and bring it to her.

Callie has always enjoyed feeding Sasha. Callie is fearless, and holds out the morsel, and Sasha stands very still, and reaches out with her lips, to engulf the tiny fingers around the food, and slowly withdraws, with the food in her mouth. Callie always appears quite pleased, and it is sometimes difficult to get her to eat enough, instead of giving away most of her food.

Peter also enjoys feeding Sasha, but his devotion to food runs deeper than Callie's, and his sharing begins only after he is full.

We have recently acquired a new grandchild whose communication, crying, causes considerable agitation in Sasha. Erik, the son of Kurt and Renee, appears to Sasha to be a very attractive puppy, and to need a thorough licking by an experienced Aunt Sasha. She stays as close to him as permitted, with intense attention.

Some of Sasha's communications appear to involve abstract thinking, involving two- and three-step charades. If we are sitting facing the deck door, we cannot see the front door. Before we installed a pet door, Sasha would trot over to the deck door and wait to be let out. When we would start for that door, Sasha would trot over to the *front* door. She has several of these charades, beginning with a general category and proceeding to the specific. She sometimes gets our attention by sitting in front of us and fixing intently on our eyes with a "death stare." Once she is acknowledged, she goes on to the next part of the dramatization, such as leading toward the door. If the stare doesn't work, she will escalate to vocalizations; if you are *really* resistant, she may gently take a finger in her mouth and pull you toward the kitchen.

She has a conviction that certain desired events, such as snack time, might be hastened if specific sequences are begun earlier.

She will therefore try to persuade Ellie to feed her in mid-afternoon, even when she is not hungry, because she knows that this is the first of a sequence that she looks forward to.

After her dish is full, she then goes out to the side deck and watches and listens for my car—she recognizes it as I stop at the mailbox at the bottom of the driveway. Then she trots to the top of the stairs from the garage and waits with a nose kiss, and then leads me into the kitchen to help me make a drink for Ellie and myself.

Of course, once the refrigerator door is open, her block of bulk cheese is there, and Sasha gets her two slices. Only when she is convinced that the snacks are over will she eat her dinner of—sob!—dog food. But she is firmly convinced of the principle of *post hoc, ergo propter hoc*, and she is prepared to hasten the process in an orderly fashion.

Transactions.

Transactional analysis was a popular field of psychology for an interval—and may still be for all I know. Sasha seems to have done graduate study in the subject. Particularly as a pup, it was obvious that certain transgressions on the part of her hosts had to be dealt with firmly. Accidentally leaving her alone in the bedroom with the door closed was invariably followed by retaliation.

The first, and still new, pair of Balley shoes I ever owned were attacked when she was only four months old, mauling the tongue. Her expensive taste in revenge cost her a spanking, since such luxury entertainment had to be discouraged, even for a princess.

It has been fascinating to watch her mature and select objects for retaliation that are more symbolic and less expensive. For example, instead of shoes or slippers, she now steals paper out of the waste basket and shreds it on the floor. She makes sure that we get the message by loudly scrambling under furniture such as a desk or a bureau, a sound that is invariably associated with a waste basket raid. (Sometimes nowadays she will do this for amusement, rather than retaliation, hoping to provoke us to take it away before she shreds it.)

Another form of retaliation for being left alone is to sleep on our bed or on a couch. Of course, Ellie is not without resources;

she has a plentiful supply of mouse traps which are left on top of the target furniture. They work quite well, even when they aren't loaded, but if Ellie forgets, Sasha knows immediately and installs herself in state. Of course, this behavior is not entirely retaliatory, since the bed is pre-warmed and smells of her family, not to mention soft and comfortable. But revenge makes it even softer and more comfortable!

Even Ed has been the target of her retaliation on occasion. On one downhill outing, we couldn't take Sasha with us, and it was Ed's turn to drive. Sasha negotiated over and over with him, wanting to get into the rear of his wagon, but she was unsuccessful. Upon our return, she refused to let Ed near her, until Ed pointedly began to pet Snidely. Sasha couldn't put up with that, and had to consent to Ed's greeting after all.

What's in a name?

I have referred to Sasha here as the princess. However, when we are climbing together, I have many more names for her. These are a little embarrassing, except that all dog lovers have this weakness—Sasha just has *more* names. Pup is probably universal, but Pretty Girl, Sashie, and Sashaty are my favorites. Ed for some time, called her Josh, which irritated, like a fingernail drawn across a blackboard, but fortunately he has mastered "Sosh."

Truth be known, her name registered with the American Kennel Club is Gunther's Kenai Sasha. Kenai (pronounced keen-eye) is a pun, of course, based on her blue-white eyes and excellent vision—the allegation by Lorenz that dogs have poor vision assuredly doesn't apply to Sasha, except when compared to her ability to hear and smell.

We chose Sasha because it sounded feminine, and there was never any doubt about that characteristic in the princess. It was a little unsettling to learn from Phil, whose major was linguistics, that Sasha was diminutive for Alexander in Russian. (His taste in names, representing Alaskan and Siberian names can be appreciated by considering his dogs' names, Ulu and Woot.) Actually, Russians also use Sasha for Alexandria, a girl's name.

Sasha the entertainer.

One of the responsibilities that Sasha takes seriously is that of entertaining Ellie and me. She is content to rest quietly for hours lying close to us, but at some point decides it is time for fun and games. She not only is playful, but she continues to think up new games on her own. She obviously has learned what works on us.

One of her most successful routines is performed while I am working at my desk in the evening. There will be a series of gentle thuds, and I turn to see a princess lying on her back, thumping her tail against the floor. After getting my attention, she places both paws over her ears and eyes, and gradually brings them forward toward her nose in a remarkably coy gesture, which inevitably is rewarded by admiring comments from dad.

A retriever Sasha isn't! If you are used to a lab or retriever who *never* tires of fetching anything thrown by his or her master, it will be quickly seen that a Siberian husky has a very different attitude. She will bring an object to you for play, and will let you take it easily the first time, but when she brings it back a second time, you will have to wrestle it away from her.

This is her favorite play, grasping a rope or bone firmly in her strong teeth, and letting you, or a canine friend, hold the other end; she will try to take it away, and expects you to do the same. If it is a rope, she will demonstrate her strength with a tug-of-war.

If a play bone tossed by me lands on the bed anywhere near a blanket she pretends that the bone is under the blanket, even if it is in plain sight. She pounces with her front feet close together, and will propel the bone under the blanket if it isn't already there, and will continue to advance in that fashion, eventually getting her nose under the blanket and biting gently anything such as a hand or foot that gets close.

The precision this breed has when using their teeth is remarkable and consistent. It is demonstrated in their vigorous play with other dogs, and in one of Sasha's favorite games, tooth wrestling with people. As a rock climber I have moderately strong fingers, and I can place the index and middle fingers in her mouth crossways to her jaw, and she clamps down gently but firmly, allowing herself to be pulled around the room by her canine teeth. She

123

never breaks the skin, even though she will usually accompany all this with ferocious growls, which she had to learn. (It is my conviction that I taught her how to growl!)

Her precise proprioception (knowledge of where her body parts are) extends to more than her teeth and jaws. On a trail, she never collides with humans, but times her passing according to the space around them.

She generally accepts the house rules that require her to keep her hind feet on the floor, unless she is suddenly moved to think that you have finally relented and have bestowed human privileges, a recurring inference for her. When she has been required to get off a couch, she will go to the place on the couch where she wants to lie, and simply puts her chin down there, and silently rolls her eyes toward me, pleading her case. It would work, too, if Ellie weren't watching!

Stalking is another of her favorite pastimes. She plays that with her canine friends as well, but with me, she prefers that I stalk her. She lies very still facing me, and I slowly circle behind her. She becomes more and more tense, until she can't stand it any longer, leaps high and turns completely around in the air, and lands in a crouch, again facing me. The turn-around leap is another of her patented moves. Her pleasure is like that of a toddler playing "getcha," or an adult who enjoys the self-imposed fright of a roller coaster ride. She particularly enjoys it if I hide behind a Korean screen in our bedroom, while she waits to see from which side I will emerge.

Sasha's playfulness is particularly endearing when we are climbing and we first reach the snow level. She doesn't roll in it or anything dumb, but seems to want me to know that she *really* appreciates me bringing her to this stuff. Then she will run back toward me, landing with her two front feet together in a pounce. She then entertains by burying her entire head under the snow, in a game of hide-and-seek, then raising her head for applause from her appreciative audience!

She has even been known to entertain strangers. Recently, in the meadow before the haystack on Mount Si, a hiker was eating lunch on a rock outcropping, overlooking a fine view. Sasha de-

Sasha and Old Dad resting on the summit of Snoqualmie Mountain in late fall. (Photo by Rüdiger Lohmann).

scended, walked just past him to the very edge, and gazed intently at the view. The hiker, noting her pose, spoke to her: "You have been watching too much television."

The scorecard.

As this story concludes, there is no end to Sasha's exploits. She is now ten years old, and has climbed a total of 188 peaks in the Cascade Range, including an early winter ascent of Mount Snoqualmie. There is an undeniable stiffness in her gait now when we leave the car after the drive home after a climb, although it lasts less time than the stiffness in Ed and me.

There has been progress in her attitude toward the danger of automobiles. One of our worst fears was that Sasha had absolutely no fear of them, since she regarded them as an extension of humans, who must love her as much as we do. This last summer, she learned that cars are like porcupines, a lesson we were more than happy for her to learn. However, the lesson was almost too much for Ellie.

On a cool but sunny morning, Ellie was gardening on the perimeter of the turn-around. Sasha was absorbing some rays, lying on the warm tarmac, when Grandma Haglund drove up in her Toyota. Sasha saw the car, of course, but was supremely confident that Grandma loved her and would carefully avoid her.

Grandma does love Sasha, but she didn't see the pup and ran over her prostrate figure. At the same instant that Sasha screamed, Ellie also screamed at Grandma to stop, which she did, but *on* Sasha!

Her wonderful princess was pinned under the car, and Ellie thought perhaps a superhuman effort might lift the Toyota, and unhesitatingly grabbed the front bumper and pulled. The one-ton vehicle barely budged, but something orthopedic in Ellie's back gave a loud snap.

Meanwhile, Sasha continued to scream; Grandma was afraid to move until she knew whether to proceed or retreat, and Ellie couldn't really see in the dark under the car, in contrast to the brilliant sunlight, and besides, it wasn't easy to bend over when your back was screaming almost as loudly as Sasha.

Finally, Sasha had scrambled out enough to reveal that only the fur of her tail was pinned, and the car could be driven off. Ellie had a very sore back for the next two weeks, Grandma was more than a little rattled, and Sasha accepted all apologies with reasonable grace. The best part was that for only the price of a few wrinkles in her fur, Sasha had learned that cars are not trustworthy, even when driven by her family.

She is a little less playful with other dogs now, particularly if they aren't *lupus*-types, and she is more responsible about wandering off. (Well, she comes back sooner!) She definitely is more obedient to direct commands, although she still insists on an appropriate delay so that she won't appear servile.

Her communication skills continue to improve. The commanding stare has given way occasionally to gestures and pointing to accomplish her goals. Most endearing are the soft sobs which she confides in my ear after I have returned after an excessive absence, particularly in the mountains when I have climbed a short section too vertical for her.

Now that Sasha is a mature husky, she is generally more affectionate to Ellie and me. Recently, I spent a terrible night with a bad cold, racked with coughing spasms. Sasha got up from her bed, came to my bedside, whined softly and kissed my nose.

I thought she wanted out, and knew that I was awake (she is careful not to wake us). When I arose, she did not head toward the door, but stayed close by me—she was simply worried about me!

The next night, after another siege of coughing, instead of coming to me, she went to Ellie's side and waked her to get her to help. Fortunately, I recovered, and we can sleep better, knowing that Sasha is on guard.

❖